EVERY MAN A KING: BY
ORISON SWETT MARDEN

WORKS BY DR. MARDEN

GETTING ON
SELF-INVESTMENT
EVERY MAN A KING
*THE OPTIMISTIC LIFE
*RISING IN THE WORLD
BE GOOD TO YOURSELF
*PUSHING TO THE FRONT
PEACE, POWER, AND PLENTY
*THE SECRET OF ACHIEVEMENT
HE CAN WHO THINKS HE CAN
THE MIRACLE OF RIGHT THOUGHT
*THE YOUNG MAN ENTERING BUSINESS

Each, 12mo, cloth, $1.00 net. By mail, $1.10
Pocket Ed., silk,   1.25 net. By mail, 1.33
Pocket Ed., leather, 1.50 net. By mail, 1.58

Titles starred are also to be had in an illustrated edition at $1.50 each, postpaid.

TALKS WITH GREAT WORKERS

12mo, cloth. Illustrated edition only, $1.50 postpaid

SUCCESS NUGGETS

16mo, cloth, 50 cents net. By mail, 58 cents
Ooze leather, 75 cents net. By mail, 83 cents

BOOKLETS

DO IT TO A FINISH   WHY GROW OLD?
   NOT THE SALARY BUT THE OPPORTUNITY

12mo. Each, 30 cents net. By mail, 35 cents

CHARACTER   ECONOMY
CHEERFULNESS   OPPORTUNITY
GOOD MANNERS   AN IRON WILL
      POWER OF PERSONALITY

12mo. Each, 30 cents net. By mail, 35 cents
With illustrations, 50 cents net. By mail, 55 cents

THOUGHTS ABOUT CHARACTER
THOUGHTS ABOUT GOOD CHEER

In envelope, ready for mailing, each, 25c net. By mail, 30c. Leather, boxed, each, 75c net. By mail, 80c

THOMAS Y. CROWELL COMPANY

Every Man a King

OR
MIGHT IN MIND-MASTERY

BY

ORISON SWETT MARDEN

Author of "Pushing to the Front," "Architects
of Fate," "The Secret of Achievement,"
and Editor of "Success"

WITH THE ASSISTANCE OF
ERNEST RAYMOND HOLMES

NEW YORK

PUBLISHERS

COPYRIGHT, 1906,
BY THOMAS Y. CROWELL & CO.

Published, September, 1906

THIRTY-FIRST THOUSAND

CONTENTS

CHAPTER I
STEERING THOUGHT PREVENTS LIFE WRECKS — PAGE 3

CHAPTER II
HOW MIND RULES THE BODY — 11

CHAPTER III
THOUGHT CAUSES HEALTH AND DISEASE — 21

CHAPTER IV
OUR WORST ENEMY IS FEAR — 33

CHAPTER V
OVERCOMING FEAR — 45

CHAPTER VI
KILLING EMOTIONS — 55

CHAPTER VII
MASTERING OUR MOODS — 67

CHAPTER VIII
UNPROFITABLE PESSIMISM — 77

CHAPTER IX
THE POWER OF CHEERFUL THINKING — 95

CHAPTER X
NEGATIVE CREEDS PARALYZE — 109

CONTENTS

CHAPTER XI
AFFIRMATION CREATES POWER ... 121

CHAPTER XII
THOUGHTS RADIATE AS INFLUENCE ... 133

CHAPTER XIII
HOW THINKING BRINGS SUCCESS ... 145

CHAPTER XIV
POWER OF SELF-FAITH OVER OTHERS ... 159

CHAPTER XV
BUILDING CHARACTER ... 167

CHAPTER XVI
STRENGTHENING DEFICIENT FACULTIES ... 177

CHAPTER XVII
GAIN BEAUTY BY HOLDING THE BEAUTY THOUGHT ... 187

CHAPTER XVIII
THE POWER OF IMAGINATION ... 193

CHAPTER XIX
DON'T LET THE YEARS COUNT ... 201

CHAPTER XX
HOW TO CONTROL THOUGHT ... 221

CHAPTER XXI
THE COMING MAN WILL REALIZE HIS DIVINITY ... 231

I. STEERING THOUGHT PREVENTS LIFE WRECKS

I. STEERING THOUGHT PREVENTS LIFE WRECKS

We build our future, thought by thought,
Or good or bad, and know it not—
Yet so the universe is wrought.
Thought is another name for fate,
Choose, then, thy destiny, and wait—
For love brings love, and hate brings hate.
—ELLA WHEELER WILCOX.

A CERTAIN man of no great learning, so runs an old legend, fell heir to a ship. He knew nothing of the sea, nothing of navigation or engineering, but the notion seized him to take a voyage and command his own ship. The ship was gotten under way, the self-appointed captain allowing the crew to go ahead with their usual duties, as the multiplicity of operations confused the amateur navigator. Once headed out to sea, however, the work grew simpler, and the captain had time to observe what was going on. As he strolled on the forward deck, he saw a man turning a big wheel, now this way, now that.

"What in the world is that man doing?" he asked.

"That's the helmsman. He is steering the ship."

"Well, I don't see any use in his fiddling away there all the time. There's nothing but water ahead, and I guess the sails can push her forward. When there's land in sight, or a ship coming head on, there'll be time enough to do steering. Put up all the sails and let her go."

The order was obeyed, and the few survivors of the wreck that followed had cause to remember the fool captain who thought a ship steered herself.

You say no such man ever existed, and you are right. That isn't admitting that no such foolishness exists, however. You wouldn't be so foolish, would you?

Think a moment. Are you not in command of something more delicate, more precious, than any ship—your own life, your own mind? How much attention are you giving to the steering of that mind? Don't you let it go pretty much as it will? Don't you let the winds of anger and passion blow it hither and thither? Don't you let chance friendships, chance reading, and aimless amusement sway your life into forms you never would have deliberately chosen? Are you really captain of

STEERING THOUGHT

your own ship, driving it to a sure harbor of happiness, peace, and success? If you are not, would you not like to become such a master of the situation? It is simpler than you perhaps think, if you will but realize certain fundamental truths and put to work your own better nature. To tell you how, and to direct your efforts is the object of this series of little talks on the use of thought in life-forming.

Considering that mind governs everything in our world, that force has been singularly neglected and misunderstood. Even when tribute has been paid to its power, it has been treated as something unalterable, a tool that could be used if one was born with the genius to do so. Of recent years, the control of thought, and its use to modify character already formed, to change even external surroundings, or at least their effect on one's self, and to bring about health, happiness, and success, have been more and more studied and understood. The possibilities of thought training are infinite, its consequences eternal, and yet few take the pains to direct their thinking into channels that will do them good, but instead leave all to chance, or rather to the myriad circumstances that buffet and compel our mental action if counter-effort be not made.

There can be no more important study, no higher duty owed to ourselves and those about us, than this of thought-control, of self-control, which results in self-development. Perhaps because thought in itself is intangible, and most of us really have so little control over it, there is an impression that direction of mind action is a difficult and abstruse affair, something that requires hard study, leisure, and book knowledge to accomplish. Nothing is further from the truth. Every person, however ignorant, however uncultured, and however busy, has within himself all that is needful, and has all the time needful, to remake his intellectual nature, his character, and practically his body and his life. Every person will have a different task, different problems to solve, and different results to aim at; but the process is practically the same, and the transformation is no more impossible for one than for another.

A sculptor's chisel in the hands of a bungler may mar the loveliest statue; in the hands of a criminal it may become a burglar's tool or a murderer's bludgeon. With the power in our hands to make or mar our natures, what reckless fools we are not to try to know how to produce beauty and harmony, happiness and success. The sculptor dares not strike random blows while gazing away from the marble. With eyes steadfast, he makes every stroke count toward the final result, and that result he has fixed in his mind and in the model he has made after his ideas. We must do likewise in chiselling our characters, forming our environment, making our lives. We must know what we want, know we can get it, and set ourselves directly at the task, never relenting or relaxing in its performance.

The difference between our thought and an ordinary tool is that we must do something with it. We cannot lay it down and say we shall strike no blow. We must think, and every thought is a blow that forges a part of our lives. Let us, therefore, resolutely determine to turn thought to good use, to the best use, and then stiffen our will to carry out that determination.

However earnestly we may set about this important task, life-long habits and set ways of thinking will make it difficult for adults. The great field for work in this direction of thought-control is with the new generation. As M. E. Carter says: " If parents and guardians would devote their energies to teaching the young under their care the lesson of thought-control instead of laying so much stress upon—and enforcing obedience to—external authority, the problem of upbringing the rising generation would be wonderfully simplified, and a much higher order of human beings would soon appear upon this planet. The child taught to hold right thoughts and to expel wrong ones by governing its own mental realm needs less and less external authority, and will grow up pure-minded and truthful because of having nothing to hide, nothing to repress. Mental control is the *only* self-control, and those who learn it early escape unhappiness and many hard experiences which darken the lives of those who fail to learn that greatest of all life's lessons."

Thus for our own sakes, and for the sakes of those tender beings whose lives are largely in our keeping, let us consider the great blessings that will flow from proper understanding and control of our own life forces.

II. HOW MIND RULES THE BODY

II. HOW MIND RULES THE BODY

It is astonishing what power our mind has over our body. Let the mind therefore always be the master.—GOETHE.

BEFORE one can do much toward controlling thought, there must be realization of its power and importance, not mere acceptance of a statement. You must feel, you must be convinced, that a bad thought harms you, that a good thought helps you. There must be no playing with fire and a careless feeling that it matters little if you are off your guard part of the time. You must know in your inmost consciousness that thought alone is eternal, that it is the master of your fate, and that the thought of every moment has its part in deciding that fate. You must feel that proper control of your own thoughts will cause all good things to come naturally to you, just as all bad things will be your portion if you misuse your God-given powers. Such realization must come through consideration of proved facts.

Thought is being recognized more and more at its proper value in the work of the world, material and moral. By people of views varying greatly in detail the power of thought is stated to be almost omnipotent in human affairs. Practical demonstrations of seemingly marvellous results are convincing unthinking and material minds. Scientific experiments, instead of destroying the claims of the thinkers, substantiate them, and give scientific explanations.

Prof. W. G. Anderson, of Yale University, succeeded in practically weighing a thought, or the result of a thought's action. A student was poised on a balance so that the centre of gravity of his body was exactly over its centre. Set to solving mathematical problems, the increased weight of blood at his head changed his centre of gravity and caused an immediate dip of the balance to that side. Repeating the nine multiplication table caused a greater displacement than repeating the table of fives, and, in general, the displacement grew greater with greater intensity of thought. Carrying the experiment further, the experimenter had the student imagine himself going through leg gymnastics. As he performed the feats mentally, one by one, the blood flowed to the limbs in quantities sufficient to tip the balance according to the movement thought of. By purely mental action the centre of gravity of the body was shifted four inches, or as much as by raising the doubled arms above the shoulders. These experiments were repeated on a large number of students with the same results.

To test still further the mastering influence of mind over muscle, the strength of the right and left arms of eleven young men was registered. The average strength of the right arms was one hundred and eleven pounds; of the left arms ninety-seven pounds. The man practised special exercises with the right hand only for one week. Tests of both arms were again made, and, while the average strength of the right arm had increased six pounds, that of the unexercised left arm had increased seven pounds. This showed clearly that the brain action connected with the gymnastics developed not only the muscles put in action, but also other muscles controlled by the same portion of the brain. This could come about only by sending blood and nervous force to the proper parts by purely mental action. Dr. Anderson says of the results:

"I can prove by my muscle-bed that the important thing in all exercises is the mental effort put forth. I can lie down on this muscle-bed and think of a jig, and though apparently my feet do not move, and actually the muscles are not active, the muscle-bed sinks toward my feet, showing that there has been a flow of blood toward the muscles, and that if I did dance a jig, the muscles would be well supplied with blood under this mental stimulus."

Sandow has long taught that bodily exercise without proper thought would do little to develop muscles, and that a very little exercise, with the mind directing it, will practically rebuild the body. Certain professors of physical culture are selling this knowledge for good prices. Professor Anderson's experiments demonstrate the truth of these statements, and further that exercise involving competition and lively interest in games does far more good than merely mechanical movements, performed without interest in gymnasiums. He says that walking is poor exercise for brain-workers, as it is so purely automatic that it does not call the blood from congested brain centres, which go on solving intellectual problems. A run, a brisk walk, with a definite object necessitating the thought of speed, will send the blood to the legs and build them up. Exercising before a mirror, watching the muscles swell with the different motions, is found to aid development.

Before these experiments, Prof. Elmer Gates, at Washington, had proved that he was able, by thinking intently of a hand when it was plunged in a basin even-full of water, and willing that the blood should flow there, to make the water overflow. Thus the amount of extra blood sent to the hand could be measured, since it corresponded to the overflowed water. Every one cannot do this on first trial; perhaps not in a hundred trials, but the mind can be trained to such control of the body.

Years ago, by experiments on the famous Beaumont, whose wound in the stomach healed leaving an orifice, physicians demonstrated the great effect of depressing or elevating emotions on digestion and other functions. A telegram announcing disaster collapsed and made feverish the follicles that were actively secreting gastric juice, and left food undigested for hours.

Recent experiments on dogs by the Russian scientist Prof. Ivan Pavlov have proved conclusively that secretion of the gastric juice in the stomach does not, as long supposed, take place automatically when saliva is secreted or when food enters the stomach. On the contrary, it is secreted when a dog is made to anticipate that it is to be fed with a much-loved food, as raw meat, even though that meat is not given to it, or, if given, is not allowed to pass into the stomach but drops out of the œsophagus by a slit made for that purpose. All manner of mechanical irritation did not avail to cause a flow of gastric juice unless there was excited an idea of pleasure in eating. If the pneumogastric nerve was severed, even this anticipated gastronomic pleasure, or the actual passage of the loved meat through the severed œsophagus, did not cause gastric secretion. The part played by the mind in what have been called mere mechanical, physical functions has been thus shown. The psychological side of digestion, as of every other manifestation in the body, is the more important.

The most wonderful result of the experiments made by Professor Gates was the discovery that certain states of mind produce chemical products in the body. He says:

"In 1879 I published a report of experiments showing that when the breath of a patient was passed through a tube cooled with ice so as to condense the volatile qualities of the respiration, the iodide of rhodopsin, mingled with these condensed products, produced no observable precipitate. But, within five minutes after the patient became angry, there appeared a brownish precipitate, which indicates the presence of a chemical compound produced by the emotion. This compound, extracted and administered to men and animals, caused stimulation and excitement. Extreme sorrow, such as mourning for the loss of a child recently deceased, produced a gray precipitate; remorse, a pink precipitate, etc. My experiments show that irascible, malevolent, and depressing emotions generate in the system injurious compounds, some of which are extremely poisonous; also, that agreeable, happy emotions generate chemical compounds of nutritious value which stimulate the cells to manufacture energy." As Professor Gates has had to point out emphatically, to counteract ridiculous statements, the color of these precipitates depends on the chemical used, but with the same chemical the emotions produce different colors.

Prof. Jacques Loeb's experiments at the University of Chicago and at Stanford University have seemed to show that thought produces phenomena similar to those of electricity, that the particles of living matter change from positive to negative and negative to positive by the influence of thought. This makes the old comparison of thought to a " telegram from the brain " all the more apt, and enlarges the conception of what the mind can do in changing bodily conditions.

III. THOUGHT CAUSES HEALTH AND DISEASE

III. THOUGHT CAUSES HEALTH AND DISEASE

"It is the spirit that maketh alive. The flesh profiteth nothing."

Every volition and thought of man is inscribed on his brain, for volition and thoughts have their beginnings in the brain, whence they are conveyed to the bodily members, wherein they terminate. Whatever, therefore, is in the mind is in the brain, and from the brain in the body, according to the order of its parts. Thus a man writes his life in his physique, and thus the angels discover his autobiography in his structure.—SWEDENBORG.

IT is not necessary to appeal to scientific experiments alone to prove the control of the mind over health and disease. Every-day experience gives ample demonstration. Striking and interesting incidents by the hundred have been collected and published by physicians, but a few will suffice.

We are so accustomed to the deadly effects of certain kinds and degrees of thought that we do not think what it is that causes illness and death. Some one dies of "shock." What does that mean? Simply that some sudden and powerful thought has so deranged the bodily mechanism that it has stopped. Fright—that is, a thought of fear—stopped the heart's action. Excitement set it beating so hard that a blood-vessel burst in the head. Sudden joy caused a rush of blood to the brain that ruptured the delicate membranes. A loved one died, and the thought of grief prevented nutrition, repair of waste, and the performance of other bodily functions dependent on normal mental condition, and the person pined away and died, from some disease the enfeebled body could not resist, or from no disease at all but the sick and mourning thought. Recently a trolley wire in London broke and fell into the street with sputtering fire. A young lady, seemingly as well as any one, was about to board a car, but, on seeing the accident, fell dead. Nothing had touched her. She had suffered no harm. She simply thought she was in danger, and thought so intensely that something gave way and separated her spirit from her body. A mind more composed, less easily startled, would have saved her life. A beautiful young lady was struck in the face by a golf stick. It broke her jaw, but that was healed in a few weeks. However, a scar was left that marred her beauty. The idea of disfigurement so preyed upon her mind that she shrank from meeting people, and melancholia became habitual. A trip to Europe, expensive treatment by specialists, did no good. The idea that she was marred and scarred took all joy from her life, all strength from her body. She soon could not leave her bed. Yet no physician was able to find any organic disease. Very silly, no doubt, but it illustrates what diseased thought can do in overcoming perfectly healthy bodily functions. Had she been able to dismiss the idea she brooded over, her health would have been restored.

Fright and grief have often blanched human hair in a few hours or a few days. Ludwig, of Bavaria, Marie Antoinette, Charles I. of England, and the Duke of Brunswick are historic examples, and every little while modern instances occur. The supposed explanation is that strong emotion has caused the formation of chemical compounds, probably of sulphur, which changed the color of the oil of the hair. Such chemical action is caused suddenly by thought instead of gradually by advancing years. Dr. Rogers says: " Many causes which affect but little the constitution, accelerate the death of the hair, more especially the depressing passions, corroding anxieties, and intense thought."

Men have died because they thought they were terribly wounded when no wound existed. The story of the medical student who was frightened to death by fellow-students, who pretended to be bleeding him, has often been told. A man who thought he swallowed a tack had horrible symptoms, including a local swelling in his throat, until it was discovered that he was mistaken. Hundreds of other cases have been verified where belief sufficed to produce great suffering and even death.

On the other hand, sickness and disease gave way before strong thought of any other kind, excitement, alarm, or great joy.

Benvenuto Cellini, when about to cast his famous statue of Perseus, now in the Loggia dei Lanzi, at Florence, was taken with a sudden fever and forced to go home and to bed. In the midst of his suffering, one of his workmen rushed in to say: " O Benvenuto, your statue is spoiled, and there is no hope whatever of saving it." Dressing hastily, he rushed to his furnace, and found his metal " caked." Ordering dry oak wood brought, he fired the furnace, fiercely working in a rain that was falling, stirred the channels, and saved his metal. He continues the story thus: "After all was over, I turned to a plate of salad on a bench there and ate with a hearty appetite and drank, together with the whole crew. Afterward I retired to my bed, healthy and happy, for it was now two hours before morning, and slept as sweetly as though I had never felt a touch of illness." His overpowering idea of saving his statue not only drove the idea of illness from his mind but also drove away the physical condition and left him well.

It is related of Muley Moluc, the Moorish leader, that, when lying ill, almost worn out by incurable disease, a battle took place between his troops and the Portuguese, when, starting from his litter at the great crisis of the fight, he rallied his army, led them to victory, and then instantly sank exhausted and expired.

The biographer of Dr. Elisha Kane says:

"I asked him for the best proved instance that he knew of the soul's power over the body. He paused a moment upon my question, as if to feel how it was put, and answered as with a spring: 'The soul can lift the body out of its boots, sir! When our captain was dying —I say dying; I have seen scurvy enough to know—every old scar in his body an ulcer—I never saw a case so bad that either lived or died, men die of it, usually long before they are as ill as he was—there was trouble aboard. There might be mutiny so soon as the breath was out of his body. We might be at each others' throats. I felt that he owed the repose of dying to the service. I went down to his bunk, and shouted in his ear, "Mutiny! Captain, mutiny!" He shook off the cadaverous stupor. "Set me up!" said he, "and order these fellows before me!" He heard the complaint, ordered punishment, and from that hour convalesced.'"

Emperor Dom Pedro, of Brazil, lying ill in Europe, was made well by a cablegram from his daughter, acting as his regent, stating that she had signed a decree abolishing slavery in his country, fulfilling a life-long plan of the sick emperor.

Whence comes the power which enables a frail, delicate woman, invalid for years, unable to wait upon herself, with hardly strength enough to walk across the floor, to rush upstairs and to drag out sleeping children from a burning home? Whence comes the strength which enables such a delicate creature to draw out furniture and bedding from a house on fire? Certainly no new strength has been added to the muscle, no new strength to the blood, but still she does what, under ordinary conditions, would have been impossible for her. In the emergency she forgets her weakness, she sees only the emergency. The danger of her darling child, the loss of her home, stares her in the face. She believes firmly, for the time, that she can do what she attempts to do, and she does it. It is changed condition of the mind, not changed blood or muscle, that gives the needed energy. The muscle has furnished the power, but the conviction of the ability to do the thing was first necessary. The fire, the danger, the excitement, the necessity of saving life and property, the temporary forgetfulness of her supposed weakness—these were necessary to work the mind to the proper state.

Evidence of this power of mind over the body is thrust upon us in many ways. The wonder is that humanity has been so long recognizing the signs and making proper deductions and application. Like the power of electricity to leap oceans through the air, carrying human messages, it has always existed, but is only beginning to be generally realized.

The part played by the mind in the curing of disease is recognized by physicians, and whole books have been written giving instances where the mind has done more than medicine or surgery. One of the highest medical authorities, Dr. William Osler, summoned by King Edward VII. from Johns Hopkins University to be Regius Professor of Medicine at Oxford University, says in the Encyclopedia Americana:

"The psychical method has always played an important, though largely unrecognized, part in therapeutics. It is from faith, which buoys up the spirits, sets the blood flowing more freely and the nerves playing their part without disturbance, that a large part of all cure arises. Despondency, or lack of faith, will often sink the stoutest constitution almost to death's door; faith will enable a spoonful of water or a bread pill to do almost miracles of healing when the best medicines have been given over in despair. The basis of the entire profession of medicine is faith in the doctor, his drugs, and his methods."

Similarly, Dr. Smith Ely Jelliffe, of Columbia University, says, in the same encyclopedia:

"Unquestionably the oldest and yet youngest therapeutic agent is suggestion. The power to heal by faith is not the special property of any sect or class, nor the exclusive right of any system. Belief in gods and goddesses, prayer to idols of wood, of stone, of gossamer fiction, faith in the doctor, belief in ourselves engendered from within or without —these are all expressions of the great therapeutic value for healing that resides in the influence of mental states on bodily functions. These will not move mountains, they cannot cure consumption; they do not influence a broken leg, nor an organic paralysis; but suggestion, in its various forms, may be, and is, one of the strongest aids to all therapeutic measures. Of its abuse by designing hypnotists, blackmailers, clairvoyants, and a motley crew of parasites, space does not permit particularization. The human mind is credulous—it believes what it wants or wills to believe—and the use of suggestion in therapeutics is one of great power for good and for evil."

In this statement Dr. Jelliffe is perhaps ultra-conservative, for he would certainly admit that the knitting of a broken bone is vitally affected by the state of mind of the patient, which has to do with all the functions of breathing, digestion, assimilation, and excretion, and a sturdy resolution has, with proper conditions of climate and hygiene, aided in the recovery from the milder stages of consumption, while even the stagnation of paralysis has been stirred into life by violent shocks to the mind and nervous system.

Long ago, Sir James Y. Simpson said: "The physician knows not, and practises not the whole extent of his art, when he neglects the marvellous influence of the mind over the body."

Churchill has given us the philosophy of health in the verse:

"The surest road to health, say what they will,
Is never to suppose we shall be ill.
Most of those evils we poor mortals know,
From doctors and imagination flow."

IV. OUR WORST ENEMY IS FEAR

IV. OUR WORST ENEMY IS FEAR

Our doubts are traitors, and make us lose the good we oft might win, by fearing to attempt.—SHAKESPEARE, *Measure for Measure*.

THOUGHT'S most deadly instrument for marring human lives is fear. Fear demoralizes character, destroys ambition, induces or causes disease, paralyzes happiness in self and others, and prevents achievement. It has not one redeeming quality. It is all evil. Physiologists now well know that it impoverishes the blood by demoralizing assimilation and cutting off nutrition. It lowers mental and physical vitality, deadens every element of success. It is fatal to the happiness of youth, and is the most terrible accompaniment of old age. Buoyancy flees before its terrifying glance, and cheerfulness cannot dwell in the same house with it.

" The most extensive of all the morbid mental conditions which reflect themselves so disastrously on the human system is the state of fear," says Dr. William H. Holcomb. " It has many degrees or gradations, from the state of extreme alarm, fright, or terror, down to the slightest shade of apprehension of impending evil. But all along the line it is the same thing—a paralyzing impression upon the centres of life which can produce, through the agency of the nervous system, a vast variety of morbid symptoms in every tissue of the body."

"Fear is like carbonic-acid gas pumped into one's atmosphere," says Horace Fletcher. "It causes mental, moral, and spiritual asphyxiation, and sometimes death—death to energy, death to tissue, and death to all growth."

Yet from our birth we live in the presence and under the dominion of this demon, fear. The child is cautioned a thousand times a year to look out for this, and to look out for that; it may get poisoned, it may get bitten, it may get killed; something terrible may happen to it if it does not do so and so. Men and women cannot bear the sight of some harmless animal or insect because, as children, they were told it would hurt them. One of the cruelest things imaginable is to impress into a child's plastic mind the terrible image of fear, which, like the letters cut upon a sapling, grows wider and deeper with age. The baleful shadows of such blasting and blighting pictures will hang over the whole life and shut out the bright sun of joy and happiness.

An Australian writer says:

"One of the worst misfortunes which can possibly happen to a growing child is to have a mother who is perpetually tormented by nervous fears. If a mother gives way to fears —morbid, minute, and all-prevailing—she will inevitably make the environment of her children one of increasing dread and timidity. The background of fear is the habit or instinct of anticipating the worst. The mother who never makes a move, or allows her children to make a move, without conjuring up a myriad of malign possibilities, imbitters the cup of life with a slow-acting poison.

"I know that thousands of boys and girls are to-day tremulous, weak, passive, unalert on the physical side, simply because they were taught in the knickerbocker stage, or earlier, to see the potency of danger in all they did or tried to do. A mother assumes a terrible responsibility when from silly fears of possible injury she forbids a child such physical abandon as will promote courage, endurance, self-reliance, and self-control."

"For more than twenty years I have made a study of criminal psychology and of infantile psychology," says Dr. Lino Ferriani. "Thousands of times I have been compelled to recognize the sad fact that at least eighty-eight per cent. of morbidly timid children could have been cured and saved in time by means of common-sense principles of psychical and physiological hygiene, in which the main factor is suggestion inspired by wholesome courage."

Not content with instilling fear of possibly real things, many mothers and most nurses invent all sorts of bugbears and bogies to frighten poor babies into obedience. They even attempt to induce sleep by telling children, "If you don't go right to sleep, a great big bear will come and eat you up!" How much sleep would a grown man get in a situation where this was a real possibility? Fear of the dark would seldom exist if parents carefully showed children that nothing is different in the dark from what it is in the light. Instead of so doing, they take pains to people the mysterious dark with every sort of ogre and monster that human imagination has been able to conjure up. Some one has well expressed in verse this cruel but too common sin against healthy-minded childhood:

OUR WORST ENEMY, FEAR

"He who checks a child with terror,
  Stops its play and stills its song,
Not alone commits an error,
  But a grievous moral wrong."

Mothers waste much energy in worrying about their children. Some of them cannot take a moment's comfort while their boys or girls are out of their sight. How many times, in imagination, have you seen your children tumble out of trees and off sheds? How many times have you pictured them drowning when they went for a sail or a skate? How often have you had visions of your boy being brought home from the base-ball or foot-ball grounds with broken limbs or scarred face? When none of these things happened, what had you to compensate for the hours of mental anguish, with consequent lowering of vitality and physical tone? Such useless imaginings of evil make many women old and haggard before their time. The worst of it is that so many think it is their duty, and a sign of their great love to worry all the time.

With fearsome and anxious mothers surrounding children with an atmosphere of dread, and suggesting to them new and unthought-of objects of fear, it is not astonishing that the whole world seems burdened and bowed down under a fearful weight of fear and anxiety. Go into almost any gathering, no matter how gay and happy the crowds seem to be, you will find, if you question any one of even the gayest, that the canker-worm of fear gnaws at the heart in some form. The fear of accident, of sickness, of poverty, of death, of some terrible misfortune, still lingers during the greatest apparent gayety. Thousands of people thus pass their lives under the shadow of fear, haunted by the dread of some vague, impending evil.

Many men and women narrow their lives by worrying over what may happen to-morrow. The family cannot afford to have any little, legitimate pleasure, to travel, or to take the leading magazines or papers. They cannot afford much-needed vacations. They must economize on clothes, on food even, and on every form of culture or recreation costing money, simply because times may be hard next year. " There may be a financial panic," urges the pessimist. " Some of the children may be sick, the times may be bad, our crops may fail, some business venture may not succeed. We can't tell what might happen, but we must prepare for the worst." The lives of hundreds of families are mutilated, sometimes utterly ruined, by this bugbear of misfortune just ahead.

One of the worst features of this parsimonious, anxious, untrustful way of living is that it stunts the development of young lives, and throws its dark shadow over the future as well as the present. A girl or boy, for instance, should go to college this year. Time flies quickly, and almost before they realize it they will be too old to go. But the father and mother assure themselves that they cannot afford any extra expense this year; the children must wait a little longer; and every year it is the same: "They must wait a little longer."

How many men and women are handicapped in their life-work, robbed of their possibilities, because lacking an education which parents, in anticipation of reverses that never came, postponed until too late?

No one should discourage proper economy and frugality, but this gloomy fear that "something may happen," this postponing enjoyment, education, culture, travel, books, innocent pleasures of every kind, until the sensibilities become hardened, until the æsthetic faculties are dead, is a disease of narrow, untrustful souls, which every sane person should combat.

Think of the millions of human creatures that God has made and placed on this glad earth, endowed with every faculty possible to enable them to enjoy life, wasting precious years in worrying and fretting lest something may happen.

How pitiful are the anxious, wrinkled faces, the gray hairs, the unhappy expressions of those who worry about possible misfortunes! Not one wrinkle in a thousand, not one gray hair in a million, has been produced by actual ills. The things which turn hair gray and plough fair faces with cruel furrows, which rob the step of elasticity, and take the buoyancy from life are bridges that never were crossed, misfortunes that never came. The sorrows and trials which actually come to us are, except in rare instances, trifling, compared with the things about which we worry, but which never come to pass.

What a waste of energy and human life is involved in this pernicious habit of anticipating evil! Think of the amount of work you could have accomplished by the mental and physical force you have expended in fearing what might happen—but which did not. Think of the wasted hours in which you planned what you would do if misfortune should come.

If we could only rid ourselves of imaginary troubles, our lives would be infinitely happier and healthier. Thus one of the greatest tasks in character-building is to eliminate, to uproot, to wipe out completely the baleful effects of fear in all its varieties of manifestation. No one can lead a naturally healthy, sunny, helpful, harmonious life while living in a fear environment. No one can hope to be entirely happy and successful without the destruction, the eradication, of the fear-germs. Were this done, the world would be gloriously changed for the better. It is the duty of every individual to conquer this common enemy in his own mind, and to do all he can to wrest other people, especially the young, from the dominion of this phantom monster. Happily, thinkers and investigators have proven that this may be done, and it is a glorious prophecy that coming generations will be taught to banish all fear, to march, clear-eyed and confident, toward the goal of perfect happiness.

V. OVERCOMING FEAR

V. OVERCOMING FEAR

Fear-thought, the arch-enemy of mankind, can be eliminated from the habit of thought—can be entirely eradicated; but not by repression.—HORACE FLETCHER.

IN setting about the overcoming of fear, we must first understand what it is we fear. It is always something that has not yet happened; that is, it is non-existent. Trouble is an imaginary something that we think of, and which frightens us with its possibility. Suppose you are afraid of yellow-fever; that is, you are afraid of the suffering caused by the disease, and especially of its probable fatal termination. As long as you have not the fever, it does not exist for you. If you have it, it has not killed you yet, and it may not do so. The most that can actually exist for you at any one time is pain and physical weakness. A state of terror aggravates every disagreeable feature of the illness and makes a fatal issue almost certain. It is because this disease is so feared that it is so often fatal, and even its contagion seems to be governed very largely by the fear people have of it, in spite of germs, and microscopic proofs of their part in the development of the disease. That is, the germs do not often affect a normal, healthy, fearless person.

During a yellow-fever epidemic at New Orleans, in the days before all the doctors had agreed that the disease is contagious, a young Northern teacher arrived at Natchez, Miss., in a high fever. Dr. Samuel Cartwright was called. The next morning he, according to Dr. William H. Holcomb, called the officers of the hotel and all the regular boarders into the parlor and made them a speech something like this:

"This young lady has yellow-fever. It is not contagious. None of you will take it from her; and if you will follow my advice, you will save this town from a panic, and a panic is the hot-bed of an epidemic. Say nothing about this case. Ignore it absolutely. Let the ladies of the house help nurse her, and take flowers and delicacies to her, and act altogether as if it were some every-day affair, unattended by danger. It will save her life, and perhaps, in the long run, many others."

The advised course was agreed to by all but one woman, who proceeded to quarantine herself in the most remote room of the hotel. The young teacher got well, and no one in the house except this terror-stricken woman took yellow-fever. Even she recovered.

"By his great reputation and his strong magnetic power," says Dr. Holcomb, "Dr. Cartwright dissipated the fears of those around him and prevented an epidemic. For this grand appreciation and successful application of a principle—the power of mind and thought over physical conditions, a power just dawning on the perception of the race—he deserves a nobler monument than any we have accorded heroes and statesmen."

Most people are afraid to walk on a narrow place high above ground. If that same narrow space were marked on a broad walk, they could keep within it perfectly, and never think of losing balance. The only dangerous thing about walking in such a place is the fear of falling. Steady-headed people are simply fearless; they do not allow the thought of possible danger to overcome them, but keep their physical powers under perfect control. An acrobat has only to conquer fear to perform most of the feats that astound spectators. For some feats, special training and development of the muscles, or of the eye and judgment, are necessary, but a cool, fearless head is all that is necessary for most.

The images that frighten a child into convulsions in a dark room do not exist for the parent. When the child is convinced that the ghosts and monsters are not real, the terror ceases. A city child who had never walked on the grass showed terror when first placed on yielding turf, and walked as gingerly as if it had been hot iron. There was nothing to be afraid of, but the child thought there was. Once the belief of danger was eradicated, the fear was gone. So it would be with grown-up fears if habit, race-thought, and wrong early training did not set us in grooves that are hard to get out of. If we could but once rise to the conviction that fear is but an image of the mind, and that it has no existence except in our consciousness, and no power to harm, except that which we give it, what a boon it would be to the human race!

Take a very common fear—that of losing one's position. The people who make their lives miserable worrying about this possible misfortune have not yet been discharged. As long as they have not, they are suffering nothing, there is no danger of want. The present situation is therefore satisfactory. If discharge comes, it is then too late to worry about its coming, and all previous worrying would have

OVERCOMING FEAR

been pure waste, doing no good, but rather weakening one for the necessary struggle to get placed again. The thing to worry about then will be that another place will not be found. If a place is found, all the worrying will again be useless. Under no circumstances can the worrying be justified by the situation at any particular time. Its object is always an imaginary situation of the future.

In overcoming your various fears, follow each one out to its logical conclusion thus, and convince yourself that at the present moment the things you fear do not exist save in your imagination. Whether they ever come to pass in the future or not, your fear is a waste of time, energy, and actual bodily and mental strength. Quit worrying just as you would quit eating or drinking something you felt sure had caused you pain in the past. If you must worry about something, worry about the terrible effects of worrying; it may help you to a cure.

Merely convincing yourself that what you fear is imaginary will not suffice until you have trained your mind to throw off suggestions of fear, and to combat all thought that leads to it. This means constant watchfulness and alert mental effort. When the thoughts of foreboding, or worry, begin to suggest themselves, not only do not indulge them, and let them grow big and black, but change your thought, think of all that tends in the opposite direction. If the fear is of personal failure, instead of thinking how little and weak you are, how ill-prepared for the great task, and how sure you are to fail, think how strong and competent you are, how you have done similar tasks, and how you are going to utilize all your past experience and rise to this present occasion, do the task triumphantly, and be ready for a bigger one. It is such an attitude as this, whether consciously assumed or not, that carries men to higher and yet higher places.

This same principle of crowding out the fear-thought by a buoyant, hopeful, confident thought can be applied to all the many kinds of fear that daily and hourly beset us. At first it will be hard to change the current of thought, to cease to dwell on sombre and depressing things. An aid in the process is often advisable. A sudden change of work to something requiring concentration of mind will often act as a switch. Recalling some humorous or pleasant incident will often " drive dull care away," as the school song has it. A very interesting or very humorous book is pretty sure to work well if one really reads with attention.

In the last analysis, all fear resolves itself into fear of death, and writers on the means of getting rid of fear dwell especially on this basic form. Death will perhaps always be a mystery, but whatever view of it be taken, a logical analysis will remove the terror of it, especially that form which makes lifeless human flesh a repulsive and terrible object. We think the feeling that Hindoos have about the flesh of animals is very queer, since to us this is most appetizing food. Our own fear of a human corpse is just as foolish as the Hindoo fear, and if we would rid ourselves of fear, we must teach ourselves so. Familiarity with the thing feared is always advisable, and frequently is quite sufficient. We know this to be true with horses, and have only to apply the matter to our own foolish fears. Horace Fletcher advises even a course in a hospital dissecting-room if nothing else will dissipate the unreasoning fear of a dead body.

"Whatever may lie beyond the tomb," says W. E. H. Lecky, "the tomb itself is nothing to us. The narrow prison-house, the gloomy pomp, the hideousness of decay, are known to the living, and the living alone. By a too common illusion of the imagination, men picture themselves as consciously dead—going through the process of corruption, and aware of it; imprisoned, with a knowledge of the fact, in the most hideous of dungeons. Endeavor earnestly to erase this illusion from your mind; for it lies at the root of the fear of death, and it is one of the worst sides of mediæval and much modern art that it tends to strengthen it. Nothing, if we truly realize it, is less real than the grave. We should be no more concerned with the after-fate of our discarded bodies than with that of the hair which the hair-cutter has cut off. The sooner they are resolved into their primitive elements the better. The imagination should never be suffered to dwell upon their decay."

Whatever the means, the task of conquering fear is the most important in character-building, and it will repay any effort. Not until this is done, and effectively, finally done, can the human soul take its proper place, rise to its God-given dominion, and progress to **higher and yet higher planes of power.**

VI. KILLING EMOTIONS

VI. KILLING EMOTIONS

Anger and worry not only dwarf and depress, but sometimes kill.—HORACE FLETCHER.

Violence is transient. Hate, wrath, vengeance are all forms of fear, and do not endure. Silent, persistent effort will dissipate them all. Be strong.—ELBERT HUBBARD.

FEAR is not the only emotion that can do us deadly harm. Weak-hearted persons are warned at peril of their lives against all unusual and disturbing emotions, but the injury to sounder persons is only of lesser degree. Many a violent paroxysm of rage has caused apoplexy and death. Grief, long-standing jealousy, and corroding anxiety are responsible for many cases of insanity. Emotion thus kills reason.

Grief is one of the best known and most recognized of these killing emotions, as has already been mentioned. Correggio is said to have died of chagrin that he received only forty ducats for a picture that is now one of the treasures of the Dresden gallery. Keats died of criticism too keen for his sensibilities, as have hundreds of other sensitive souls. Instances are not rare of young girls dying from disappointment in love.

Even joy kills when its impact is too sudden. The daily papers sometimes tell of an aged parent dying on the sudden arrival of a long-lost child, or of the news of a great good fortune having a fatally exciting effect. A man in Paris died when his number proved a winning one in a lottery. Surprise at her son's bringing home a bride killed Mrs. Corea, of Copake, N. Y., in five minutes.

Even if the emotion is not strong enough to kill, its effect may be most injurious. A fit of anger will destroy appetite, check digestion, and unsettle the nerves for hours, or even days. It upsets the whole physical make-up, and, by reaction, the mental and the moral. Just as it changes a beautiful face to a hideous one, it changes the whole disposition for the time being. Anger in a mother may even poison a nursing child. Extreme anger or fright may produce jaundice, and these or other emotions sometimes cause vomiting.

Jealousy will upset the entire system, and is one of the most deadly enemies to health, happiness, and success. Victims of jealousy oftentimes lose their health entirely until the cause is removed, and become so demoralized mentally that they commit murder or suicide, or go insane. A standing head-line in Paris newspapers is "*Drames Passionels*" (Tragedies from Passion). A strong, continual hatred will sometimes not only destroy digestion, assimilation, and peace of mind, but also absolutely ruin character.

These bodily effects of the emotions, and many others, are in part due to certain chemical products formed in the body by the emotions. Medical men say that they are analogous to the venom of poisonous snakes, which is likewise secreted under the influence of fear and anger. The snake has a sac in which to store the venom; we have none, and it spreads through all the tissues in spite of efforts to eliminate it.

Prof. Elmer Gates, who has gone further than any other scientist into the investigation of emotions, says:

"It need not surprise any one that the emotions of sadness and pain and grief affect the bodily secretions and excretions, because every one must have observed that during these depressing emotions the respiration goes on at a slower rate, the circulation is retarded, digestion is impaired, the cheeks become pale, the eyes grow lustreless, and so forth."

By various means and ingenious instruments, testing the "fatigue point," the "reactionary period," etc., Professor Gates determined that a person is capable of greater muscular, intellectual, and volitional activity under the influence of happy moods than under the influence of depressing emotions.

"The system makes an effort to eliminate the metabolic products of tissue-waste," says Professor Gates, "and it is therefore not surprising that during acute grief tears are copiously excreted; that during sudden fear the bowels are moved and the kidneys are caused to act, and that during prolonged fear the body is covered with a cold perspiration; and that during anger the mouth tastes bitter—due largely to the increased elimination of sulphocyanates. The perspiration during fear is chemically different, and even smells different than during a happy mood."

After pointing out the part elimination of poisons takes in bodily economy, Professor Gates continues:

"Now it can be shown in many ways that the elimination of waste products is retarded by the sad and painful emotions; nay, worse than that, these depressing emotions directly augment the amount of these poisons. Conversely, the pleasurable and happy emotions, during the time they are active, inhibit the poisonous effects of the depressing moods, and cause the bodily cells to create and store up vital energy and nutritive tissue products.

"Valuable advice may be deduced from these experiments; during sadness and grief an increased effort should be volitionally made to accelerate the respiration, perspiration, and kidney action, so as to excrete the poison more rapidly. Take your grief into the open air, work till you perspire; by bathing wash away the excreted eliminates of the skin several times daily; and above all, use all the expedients known to you—such as the drama, poetry, and the other fine arts, and direct volitional dirigation, to educe the happy and pleasurable emotions. Whatever tends to produce, prolong, or intensify the sad emotions is wrong, whether it be dress, drama, or what not. Happiness is a means rather than an end—it creates energy, promotes growth and nutrition, and prolongs life. The emotions and other feelings give us all there is of enjoyment in life, and their scientific study and rational training constitute an important step in the art of using the mind more skilfully and efficiently. By proper training the depressing emotions can be practically eliminated from life, and the good emotions rendered permanently dormant. All this is extremely optimistic."

Nursing grief month after month, or year after year, as so many do, is a crime against oneself, and against all others with wh m one comes in contact. It does absolutely no good to anybody, least of all to the grieving person, who certainly is no happier for it. The person dead or gone away can take no pleasure in the perpetual mourning, and everybody who lives with the mourner is depressed and injured by the pall of lugubriousness. Such mourning is only self-pity, a form of selfishness. Pleasure and comfort from a certain source may have gone out of your life, but why not live in the joyous memory of what was once enjoyed, rather than make yourself and many others miserable because you cannot have a constant supply of this same pleasure? What would you think of a tourist who came back from Switzerland weeping and mourning because he could not always remain in some beautiful valley and enjoy the loveliest view he had ever seen? You expect his eye to grow bright and his manner animated as he tells of the beauty he saw and the pleasure he felt.

"In this connection," says Horace Fletcher, "the suggestion should be urged that separation—as in death—is unessential as compared with the privilege of having known a beloved one, and that appreciation and gratitude should always outweigh regret in relation to an inevitable change.

"The attitude toward the separation called death should be such as to induce the thought, and even the expression: 'Pass on, beloved; enter into the better state which all the processes of nature teach are the result of every change; it will soon be my time to follow; my happiness at your preferment attend you; my love is blessed with that happiness; and what you have been to me remains, and will remain forever.'"

Anger has many forms and many causes, but, as Horace Fletcher has shown, it has its root in fear. One is angry because one fears bodily harm, or injury to material interests, or deprivation of some enjoyed blessing, or injury to reputation or friendship through something that some one has said or done. The self-confident, fearless, composed person does not get angry, though suffering all the trials and vexations that make another person "fly all to pieces" a dozen times a day. That common expression, by the way, exactly describes the effect of anger. One's mental and physical harmony does " fly all to pieces," and is a long time getting patched up again.

Self-control is of course the preventive of anger. Logic and deliberation in judging of incidents and their effect on one are conducive to self-control. A common excitant to anger is an epithet, the calling of a name. Think just what this is, and you must decide that it is silly to lose one's temper over it. You are angry really because you are afraid somebody may believe the characterization is true. Were you absolutely sure of yourself and your reputation, the epithet would have no more effect than the barking of a dog, or a word in some foreign language that you did not understand. It has no real effect at all, only what you allow it to have in your own mind. It does not alter the facts in the case in the least. The wise attitude is that taken by Mirabeau, who, when speaking at Marseilles, was called " calumniator, liar, assassin, scoundrel." He said, " I wait, gentlemen, till these amenities be exhausted."

Anger because some one has done work wrong does not help matters any. It does not undo the mistake, or make the erring one not less likely to repeat the error than would a careful showing of what is wrong, and the proper method. Your own energy could be far more profitably spent than in a fit of temper.

Whatever the cause of anger, it will usually be found to be trivial. A proof is that quick-tempered people are always apologizing the next day, when the matter looks very different. Cultivate the habit of forming this "tomorrow" judgment to-day, and your angry explosions will be reduced to a minimum. Cultivate optimism in general, and particularly the love-thought, toward all people with whom you come in contact, and you will soon find it hard to be angry with any of them. Jealousy and hatred will disappear by the cultivation of the same attitude of mind. Whatever the killing emotion that you are allowing to destroy your happiness and shorten your life, the remedy can be found within yourself, in your own thinking and acting. Long ago Epictetus practised the remedy and said:

"Reckon the days in which you have not been angry. I used to be angry every day; now every third day; then every third and fourth day; and if you miss it so long as thirty days, offer a sacrifice of thanksgiving to God."

VII. MASTERING OUR MOODS

VII. MASTERING OUR MOODS

A character is a man who knows what he wants; who does not allow his temper and moods to govern him, but acts on firm principles.—TREU.

WHEN things go hard with you, when everything seems to go against you, when you are thwarted on every side, when the sky is dark and you can see no light, that is just the time to exhibit your mettle, to show of what stuff you are made. If there is anything in you, adversity will bring it out. What a man does in spite of circumstances, rather than because of them, is the measure of his success ability.

When you get up in the morning feeling blue and discouraged because disagreeable things confront you, make up your mind firmly that, come what may, you will make that particular day a "red-letter" day in your life. Then, instead of a probable failure and the loss of a day, you will at least accomplish infinitely more than you would have done if you had given way to your depressing mood.

Man is naturally a lazy animal, and when

things go hard with him the temptation to slip over or get around the difficult place is very strong. But this is not the way to kill the dragon that dogs your footsteps and robs you of your happiness. Do not shake off or avoid your work; do not go around obstacles —go through them. Seize the dragon by the head and strangle him.

"Above all," says Frank C. Haddock, in "The Power of Will," "anger, irritation, jealousy, depression, sour feelings, morose thoughts, worry, should be forever banished from the mind by the resolute, masterful will. All these are physiological devils. They not only disturb the mind, but also injure the body by developing poisonous and distorting cells. They prevent an even circulation. The poisons which they generate are deadly in the extreme. They flatten and tear asunder cells of nervous tissue. They induce permanent physiological states which are inimical to vigorous will. They dispel hopefulness, and obscure high motives, and lower the mental tone. They should be cast out of life with the resolution that as aliens they shall always be treated. They may be throttled and slaughtered and locked absolutely out of your existence. Whoever will accomplish these great results will

MASTERING OUR MOODS

discover a growth of will adequate to every normal demand."

If you are morose, moody, or despondent; if you have the habit of worrying or fretting about things, or any other fault that hinders your growth, you will never rid yourself of it by brooding over it. Nothing is more certain than that nursing such feelings aggravates them. But if the sufferer will try to change the current of his thought by calling up some happy memory, looking on some beautiful object in art or in nature, reading from some helpful, uplifting book, the "blues" will soon vanish. Sunshine will take the place of gloom, and joy of sadness. As Mrs. Wiggs says: "The way to get cheerful is to smile when you feel bad, to think about somebody else's headache when your own is 'most bustin', to keep on believin' the sun is a-shinin' when the clouds is thick enough to cut."

One of the brightest and most cheerful women I ever knew told me that she was prone to fits of depression or the blues, but that she learned to conquer them by forcing herself to sing a bright, joyous song, or to play a lively air on the piano, whenever she felt an "attack" coming on.

The expelling power of a contrary emotion is practically perfect, if the new thought be stronger than the old.

"The only cure for indolence is work," says Rutherford; "the only cure for selfishness is sacrifice; the only cure for unbelief is to shake off the ague of doubt by doing Christ's bidding; the only cure for timidity is to plunge into some dreadful duty before the chill comes on." Similarly, the cure for bad moods is to summon good ones to fill one's whole mind and thought. It requires a strong effort of will, but the only way to conquer any fault is to think persistently of the opposite virtue, and to practise it until it is yours by the force of habit. Hold just the opposite thought from that which depresses you, and you will naturally reverse the mood. The imagination has great power to change an unpleasant thought or experience. When you are the victim of vicious moods, just say to yourself: "This is all unreal; it has nothing to do with my higher and better self, for the Creator never intended me to be dominated by such dark pictures." Persistently recall the most delightful experiences, the happiest days of your life. Hold persistently in the mind such things as you have enjoyed; drive out the failure-thoughts by thinking of the successful things you have accomplished. Persistently hold joyous thoughts when sadness threatens. Call hope to your aid, and picture a bright, successful future. Surround yourself with such happy thoughts for a few minutes, and you will be surprised to see how all the ghosts of blackness and gloom—all thoughts which have worried and haunted you—have gone out of sight. They cannot bear the light. Light, joy, gladness, and harmony are your best protectors; discord, darkness, and sickness cannot exist where they are. As a writer in the *Magazine of Mysteries* says: " Our troubles can stand anything better than indifference and ridicule. When we separate ourselves from them and forget them for things of greater interest, or when, in our own minds, we turn their insignificance to derision, they speedily slink away abashed and hide their ' diminished heads.' "

Until we can master our moods, we can never do our best work. No man who is at the mercy of his moods is a free man. He only is free who can rise to his dominion in spite of his mental enemies. If a man must consult his moods every morning to see whether he can do his best work, or only some unimportant task during the day; if he must look at his mental thermometer when he rises, to see whether his courage is rising or falling, he is a slave; he cannot be successful or happy.

How different is the outlook of the man who feels confident every morning that he is going to do a man's work, the very best that he is capable of, and that no mood or outward circumstance can hinder that accomplishment. How superbly he carries himself who has no fear, no doubt, no anxiety.

It is true that this supreme self-dominion, which marks one calm, powerful soul in a million who fret and stew and are mastered by their moods, is one of the last lessons of culture, but it is a prerequisite to great achievement, and by proper effort it is possible to all. When this is attained, we need no longer env those serene souls who impress us with . sense of power, of calm, unhesitating assurance, who travel toward their goal with the rhythm and majesty of the celestial bodies. They are only those who have learned to think correctly, to master their moods and, with them, men and circumstances; and we can be like them if we will.

Training under pressure is the finest discipline in the world. You know **what is right and what you ought to do, even when you do** not feel like doing it. This is the time to get a firm grip on yourself, to hold yourself steadily to your task, no matter how hard or disagreeable it may be. Keep up this rigid discipline day after day and week after week, and you will soon learn the art of arts—perfect self-mastery.

VIII. UNPROFITABLE PESSIMISM

VIII. UNPROFITABLE PESSIMISM

The universe pays every man in his own coin; if you smile, it smiles upon you in return; if you frown, you will be frowned at; if you sing, you will be invited into gay company; if you think, you will be entertained by thinkers; if you love the world, and earnestly seek for the good therein, you will be surrounded by loving friends, and nature will pour into your lap the treasures of the earth.—ZIMMERMAN.

ONSIDERING how unprofitable such efforts are, it is surprising how many people make a business of looking for trouble, of cultivating and coaxing it, and running to meet it. They find the thing they look for. No one ever looked for trouble yet without finding plenty of it. This is because one can make trouble of anything if the mind is set that way. It is said that during the development of the West, in the days of rough frontier life, the men who always went armed with pistols, revolvers, and bowie-knives always got into difficulties, while the men who never carried arms, but trusted to their own good sense, self-control, tact, and humor, rarely had trouble. The incident that

meant a shooting affray to the armed man was merely a joke to the more sensible unarmed men. It is just so with the seekers for ordinary trouble. By constantly holding discouraged, dejected, melancholy, gloomy thoughts, they make themselves receptive to all that depresses and destroys. What to a cheerful person would be a trifling incident, to be laughed at and dismissed from the mind, becomes, in the minds of the croakers, a thing of dire portent, an occasion for unutterable gloom and foreboding.

Most unhappy people have gradually become so by forming the habit of unhappiness, complaining about the weather, finding fault with their food, with crowded cars, and with disagreeable companions or work. The habit of complaining, of criticising, of fault-finding or grumbling over trifles, the habit of looking for shadows, is one most unfortunate to contract, especially in early life, for after a while the victim becomes a slave. All of the impulses become perverted, until the tendency to pessimism, to cynicism, is chronic.

There are specialists in these trouble-seekers. Thousands of people go looking for disease. They keep on hand antidotes for malaria, and something for colds, and medicine for every

UNPROFITABLE PESSIMISM

possible ailment, and they are sure they will all come sometime. When they take a journey across the continent or to Europe they carry a regular drug-store with them, a remedy for every supposed ill that they are likely to strike; and, strange to say, these people are always feeling ill, they are always having colds, and catching contagious diseases. Others, who never anticipate trouble, who are always believing the best instead of the worst, will go abroad and never take remedies with them, and they rarely have any trouble.

Some people are always looking for malaria, they are always snuffing about for sewer gas and for impure air; the locality where they live must be unhealthy, too high or too low, too sunny or too shady. If they have any little ache or pain, they are sure it is malaria. Of course they eventually get it because they looked for it, they anticipated it, they expected it. They would be disappointed if they found they were mistaken. The fact is that the only thing that is wrong is their own minds. If there is malaria in the mind, if there is miasma in the thought, these things will appear in the body. It is only a question of time.

Some of these trouble-seekers fix on the stomach as the storm-centre of misfortune.

They have elaborate mental charts of what "agrees with" them and what "disagrees with" them, and are always secretly hoping to be able to find some new indigestible viand. They swallow a bit of dyspepsia with every mouthful of food, for they feel sure that everything they eat will hurt them. The suspicious thought, the fear thought, reacts upon the digestion, demoralizes the gastric juice or prevents its secretion entirely, and, of course, there is trouble.

Some of these peculiar individuals find the air the most prolific source of their quarry. The whole French nation is continually looking for trouble from this source. An American in Paris who leaves a bedroom window open is warned against sore eyes, pneumonia, colds, and sudden death. If there is a window open anywhere, these suspecters of aerial mischief expect a cold, and are sure to get it. The very fear, the very anxiety, demoralizes the natural resisting power of the body and makes it susceptible.

If there is a contagious disease anywhere in the neighborhood, the trouble-expecters are sure to contract it. If one of the children coughs, or has a little too much color in the cheek, or does not feel hungry, they are certain that the dreaded disease must have begun its deadly work.

The saddest cases of all, perhaps, are those who have a fixed idea that some disease, usually supposed to be inherited, will ultimately kill them. The self-convinced victims of weak lungs, weak hearts, weak stomachs brood and dwell upon their threatened physical disasters, making them enter into every plan and calculation of life, throwing their pall over every activity of the family. All that thousands of such people need to be well and happy is a better mental state, a buoyant, hopeful attitude and the activity that would come with such a philosophy. These people are the prey of quacks of every kind, they are the "dope fiends" that swallow our millions of gallons of concoctions whose advertisements disgust the eye of every newspaper reader, they support many a fashionable physician in luxury, they make life tenfold more miserable than by any standard of right it ought to be. I wish that I had the power to stir the inmost soul of all these people to realize how much their own fate lies in the control of their own thoughts, how effort of will, by helping them to hold the healing, life-giving thought, might enable them to throw off every hampering ailment, physical and mental, and make their lives the grand expression of the divinity that is the essence of us all.

Certain people are always complaining of their hard lot and poverty. They go about with disaster written in their very faces; they are walking advertisements of their own failures, their own listless, nerveless, lifeless inactivity; they are always talking, but never doing.

I know a bright, energetic young man who has started in business for himself, but who has formed a most unfortunate habit of talking down his business to everybody. When anybody asks him how his business is getting along he says: " Poorly, poorly; no business; doing absolutely nothing; just barely making a living; no money in it; I wish I could sell out; I made a great mistake in going into this line of business; I would have been a great deal better off on salary." This man has formed such a habit of talking his business down that even when business is good, he still calls it poor. He radiates a discouraging atmosphere, he flings out discouraging suggestions, and makes you feel tired and disgusted that a young man of such promise and such possi-

UNPROFITABLE PESSIMISM

bilities should so drown his prospects and strangle his ambition.

This habit is especially unfortunate in an employer, because it is contagious; it destroys the confidence of the employees in him and in the business. People do not like to work for a pessimist. They thrive in a cheerful, optimistic atmosphere, and will do more and better work there than in one of discouragement and depression. The man who talks his business down cannot possibly do so well as the man who talks his business up. The habit of talking everything down sets the mind toward the negative side, the destructive side, instead of toward the positive and creative, and is fatal to achievement. It creates a discordant environment. No man can live upward when he is talking downward.

The imagination, wrongly used, is one of our worst foes. I know people who live in perpetual unhappiness and discomfort because they imagine they are being abused, slighted, neglected, and talked about. They think themselves the target for all sorts of evils, the object of envy, jealousy, and all kinds of ill will. The fact is, most such ideas are delusions and have no reality whatever.

Now this is a most unfortunate state of

mind to get into. It kills happiness, it demoralizes usefulness, it throws the mind out of harmony, and life itself becomes unsatisfactory.

People who think such thoughts make themselves perpetually wretched by surrounding themselves with an atmosphere reeking with pessimism. They always wear black glasses, which make everything around them seem draped in mourning; they see nothing but black. All the music of their lives is set to the minor key; there is nothing cheerful or bright in their world.

These people have talked poverty, failure, hard luck, fate, and hard times so long that their entire being is imbued with pessimism. The cheerful qualities of the mind have atrophied from neglect and disuse, while their pessimistic tendencies have been so overdeveloped that their minds cannot regain a normal, healthy, cheerful balance.

These people carry a gloomy, disagreeable, uncomfortable influence with them wherever they go. Nobody likes to converse with them, because they are always telling their stories of hard luck and misfortune. With them, times are always hard, money scarce, and society "going to the bad." After a while they become pessimistic cranks, with morbid minds, really partially unbalanced, and people avoid them as they would miasmatic swamps, full of chills and fever.

Sometimes a whole household becomes infected by the presence of one morose, discontented member, and its peace is ruined. Such a contrary person is always out of harmony with his environment, has no pleasure himself, and, as far as he is able, prevents others from having any. Such states of mind not only induce disease, but also prevent benefit from ordinary curative processes. George C. Tenney, from experience in a sanatorium, writes:

"To help a person who is at 'outs' with everything and everybody is like trying to save a drowning man who is determined to drown. Some people spend most of their time in hunting themselves over for some new ailment, and when they have found it they are the most happy that they ever are. Immediately they hang it about their necks, where it becomes an additional millstone to drag them down. Nothing does so much to obstruct the work of restoring normal conditions as for the individual to wage continual war with his situation and surroundings. Giving medicine or treatment to a person whose mind is in the turmoil of discontent is like pouring water into heated oil. Irritation and disturbance is the consequence. Healing is the work of divine power, and in the use of divinely appointed means for the recovery of health it is as necessary to be in harmony with the application of those means as though the Divine Master were himself applying the means. A good and wise Providence is seeking to work out for us a noble end; and contentment means being in harmony with the work that is being done for us, whether that work be agreeable to our feelings or not."

"It matters not what may be the cause of the trouble in the anxious mind," says Dr. A. J. Sanderson, "the results upon the body are the same. Every function is weakened, and under the continual influence of a depressed state of mind, they degenerate. Especially is this true if any organ of the body is handicapped by weakness from any other cause. The combination of the two influences will soon lead to actual disease.

"The greatest barrier in the way of the healing process, especially if the malady be one that is accompanied by severe pain, is the mental depression that is associated with it and often becomes a factor of the disease. It stands in the way of recovery sometimes more than do the physical causes, and obliterates from the consciousness of the individual the wonderful healing power of nature, so essential to recovery."

A most injurious and unpleasant way of looking for trouble is fault-finding, continual criticism of other persons. Some people are never generous, never magnanimous toward others. They are stingy of their praise, showing always an unhealthy parsimony in their recognition of merit in others, and critical of their every act.

Don't go through life looking for trouble, for faults, for failures, for the crooked, the ugly, and the deformed; don't see the distorted man—see the man that God made. Just make up your mind firmly at the very outset in life that you will not criticise or condemn others, or find fault with their mistakes and shortcomings. Fault-finding, indulging in sarcasm and irony, picking flaws in everything and everybody, looking for things to condemn instead of to praise, is a very dangerous habit to oneself. It is like a deadly worm which gnaws at the heart of the rosebud or fruit, and will make your own life gnarled, distorted, and bitter.

No life can be harmonious and happy after this blighting habit is once formed. Those who always look for something to condemn ruin their own characters and destroy their normal integrity.

We all like sunshiny, bright, cheerful, hopeful people; nobody likes the grumbler, the fault-finder, the backbiter, the slanderer. The world likes Emerson, not Nordau; likes the man who sees longevity in his cause and good in the future, who believes the best and not the worst of people. Idle gossipers, serpent tongues, people who give vent to their tempers, get only momentary satisfaction, and ever afterward they are tormented by their own ugly natures and then wonder why another person enjoys his life and they do not enjoy theirs.

It is just as easy to go through life looking for the good and the beautiful, instead of the ugly; for the noble instead of the ignoble; for the bright and cheerful instead of the dark and gloomy; the hopeful instead of the despairing; to see the bright side instead of the dark side. To set your face always toward the sunlight is just as easy as to see always the shadows, and it makes all the difference in your character between content and discon-

UNPROFITABLE PESSIMISM

tent, between happiness and misery, and in your life, between prosperity and adversity, between success and failure.

Learn to look for the light, then. Positively refuse to harbor shadows and blots, and the deformed, the disfigured, the discordant. Hold to those things that give pleasure, that are helpful and inspiring, and you will change your whole way of looking at things, will transform your character in a very short time.

A great many people think they would be happy if they were only in different circumstances, when the fact is that circumstances have little, if anything, to do with one's temperament or disposition to enjoy the world.

I know people who have lost their best friends, who have all their lives been apparently unfortunate, have struggled against odds and have themselves been invalids, and yet they have borne up bravely through it all, and have been cheerful, hopeful, inspiring to all who knew them.

You who are always unhappy, who are always grumbling about your circumstances, hard luck, and poverty, must remember that thousands of people would be happy in precisely your condition.

If you have been in the habit of talking down your business, the times, your friends, and everything, just reverse the process, talk everything up, and see how soon your changed thought will change the atmosphere about you and improve your conditions.

A strong, positive man does not allow himself to talk and think negatives. He does not say " I can't "; it is always " I can "; he does not say " I will try the thing," but " I will do it." " Cant's " have ruined more boys and young men and young women than almost anything else, for to get into the negative habit, the doubting habit, tends to keep them down. They are fastening bonds of servitude around themselves, and will not be able to counteract their influence unless they reverse their thinking, talking, and acting.

Perfect faith is the child of optimism and harmony. The pessimist atmosphere is always deadly to health and fatal to business as well as morals. The balanced soul is never suspicious, does not expect trouble, but quite the reverse. He knows that health and harmony are the everlasting facts, that disease and discord are but the absence of the opposites, as darkness is not an entity in itself, only the absence of light. Get yourself in balance, and life will look and be different to you.

> *"Brooding o'er ills, the irritable soul*
>   *Creates the evils feared, and hugs its pain.*
> *See thou some good in every sombre whole,*
> *And, viewing excellence, forget life's dole,*
>   *In will the last sweet drop of joy to drain."*

IX. THE POWER OF CHEERFUL THINKING

IX. THE POWER OF CHEERFUL THINKING

Optimism is the faith that leads to achievement; nothing can be done without hope.—HELEN KELLER.

The men whom I have seen succeed best in life have always been cheerful and hopeful men, who went about their business with a smile on their faces, and took the changes and chances of this mortal life like men, facing rough and smooth alike as it came.—CHARLES KINGSLEY.

THE cheerful man has a creative power which the pessimist never possesses. There is nothing which will so completely sweeten life and take out its drudgery, nothing that will so effectively ease the jolts on the road, as a sunny, hopeful, optimistic disposition. With the same mental ability, the cheerful thinker has infinitely more power than the despondent, gloomy thinker. Cheerfulness is a perpetual lubricator of the mind; it is the oil of gladness which dispels friction, worries, anxieties, and disagreeable experiences. The life machinery of a cheerful man does not wear out or grind away as rapidly as that of one whose moods and temper scour and wear the delicate bearings and throw the entire machinery out of harmony.

"In the maintenance of health and the cure of disease cheerfulness is a most important factor," says Dr. A. J. Sanderson. "Its power to do good like a medicine is not an artificial stimulation of the tissues, to be followed by reaction and greater waste, as is the case with many drugs; but the effect of cheerfulness is an actual life-giving influence through a normal channel, the results of which reach every part of the system. It brightens the eye, makes ruddy the countenance, brings elasticity to the step, and promotes all the inner forces by which life is sustained. The blood circulates more freely, the oxygen comes to its home in the tissues, health is promoted, and disease is banished."

A farmer in Alabama eight or ten years ago, subject to lung trouble, had a hemorrhage while ploughing one day, and lost so much blood that he was told by his physician that he would die. He merely said that he was not ready to die yet, and lingered for a long time, unable to get up. He gained strength, and finally could sit up, and then he began to laugh at anything and everything. He persisted in his hilarity, even when well people could see nothing to laugh at, and gained constantly. He became robust and strong. He says he is sure that if he had not laughed continually he would have died.

A great many people have brought sick, discordant bodies back into harmony by "the laugh cure," by substituting cheerfulness for fretting, worrying, and complaining. Every time one complains or finds fault, he is only acknowledging the power of his enemies to hold him down, to make his life uncomfortable and disagreeable. The way to get rid of these enemies of happiness, is to deny their existence, to drive them out of the mind, for they are only delusions. Harmony, health, beauty, success—these are the realities; their opposites are only the absence of the real.

"I try as much as I can," said a great philosopher, "to let nothing distress me, and to take everything that happens as for the best. I believe that this is a duty and that we sin in not so doing."

Similarly Sir John Lubbock has said:

"I cannot, however, but think that the world would be better and brighter if our teachers would dwell on the Duty and Happiness, as well as on the Happiness and Duty;

for we ought to be as cheerful as we can, if only because to be happy ourselves is the most effectual contribution to the happiness of others."

Nothing makes for one's own health and happiness so much as a serene mind. When the mind is self-poised and serene, every faculty and function falls into line and works normally. There is equilibrium and health everywhere in the body. The serene mind can accomplish infinitely more than the disturbed and discordant.

*"A serene intentness will always prevail,
Though bluster and bustle will often fail."*

The work turned out by a calm, balanced mind is healthy and strong. There is a vigor and naturalness about it which is not found in that done by a one-sided man, a mind out of balance. Serenity never dwells with discontent, with anxiety, with over-ambition. It never lives with the guilty, but dwells only with a clear conscience; it is never found apart from honesty and square dealing, or with the idle or the vicious.

The sunny man attracts business success; everybody likes to deal with agreeable, cheer-

CHEERFUL THINKING

ful people. We instinctively shrink from a crabbed, cross, contemptible character, no matter how able he may be. We would rather do a little less business or pay a little more for our goods and deal with an optimist.

The great business world of to-day is too serious, too dead in earnest. Life in America is the most strenuous ever experienced in the history of the world. There is a perpetual need of relief from this great tension, and a sunny, cheerful, gracious soul is like an ocean breeze in sultry August, like the coming of a vacation. We welcome it because it gives us at least temporary relief from the strenuous strain. Country store-keepers look forward for months to the visits of jolly, breezy travelling men, and their wholesale houses profit by their good nature. Cheerful-faced and pleasant-voiced clerks can sell more goods and attract more customers than saucy, snappy, disagreeable ones. Promoters, organizers of great enterprises, must make a business of being agreeable, of harmonizing hostile interests, of winning men's good opinion. Newspaper men, likewise, depend on making friends to gain *entrée*, to get interviews, to discover facts, and to find news. All doors fly open to the sunny man, and he is invited to enter when the disagreeable, sarcastic, gloomy man has to break open the door to force his way in. Many another business is founded on courtesy, cheerfulness, and good humor.

Employees can often make their situations easier, get more salary, and win promotion by always being cheerful and bright, besides having a pleasant, happy time themselves. Emory Belle tells how this worked in her own case:

"I started out to my work one morning, determined to try the power of cheerful thinking (I had been moody long enough). I said to myself: 'I have often observed that a happy state of mind has a wonderful effect upon my physical make-up, so I will try its effect upon others, and see if my right thinking can be brought to act upon them.' You see I was curious. As I walked along, more and more resolved on my purpose, and persisting that I was happy, that the world was treating me well, I was surprised to find myself lifted up, as it were; my carriage became more erect, my step lighter, and I had the sensation of treading on air. Unconsciously, I was smiling, for I caught myself in the act once or twice. I looked into the faces of the women I passed and there saw so much trouble and anxiety, discontent, even to peevishness, that my heart went out to them, and I wished I could impart to them a wee bit of the sunshine I felt pervading me.

"Arriving at the office, I greeted the bookkeeper with some passing remark, that for the life of me I could not have made under different conditions; I am not naturally witty; it immediately put us on a pleasant footing for the day; *she* had caught the reflection. The president of the company I was employed by was a very busy man and much worried over his affairs, and at some remark that he made about my work I would ordinarily have felt quite hurt (being too sensitive by nature and education); but this day I had determined nothing should mar its brightness, so replied to him cheerfully. His brow cleared, and there was another pleasant footing established, and so throughout the day I went, allowing no cloud to spoil its beauty for me or others about me. At the kind home where I was staying the same course was pursued, and, where before I had felt estrangement and want of sympathy, I found congeniality and warm friendship. People will meet you halfway if you will take the trouble to go that far.

"So, my sisters, if you think the world is

not treating you kindly, don't delay a day, but say to yourselves: ' I am going to keep young in spite of the gray hairs; even if things do not always come my way I am going to live for others, and shed sunshine across the pathway of all I meet.' You will find happiness springing up like flowers around you, will never want for friends or companionship, and above all the peace of God will rest upon your soul."

The world is too full of sadness and sorrow, misery and sickness; it needs more sunshine; it needs cheerful lives which radiate gladness; it needs encouragers who shall lift and not bear down; who shall encourage, not discourage.

Who can estimate the value of the sunny soul who scatters gladness and good cheer wherever he goes, instead of gloom and sadness? Everybody is attracted to these cheerful faces and sunny lives, and repelled by the gloomy, the morose, the sad. We envy people who radiate cheer wherever they go, who fling out gladness from every pore. Money, houses, lands, look contemptible beside such a disposition. The ability to radiate sunshine is a greater power than beauty, than mere mental accomplishments.

CHEERFUL THINKING

Oh, what riches live in a sunny soul! What a blessed heritage is a sunny nature, able to fling out sunshine wherever it goes, able to scatter the shadows and to lighten sorrow-laden hearts, having power to send cheer into despairing souls. And if, haply, this heritage is combined with a superb manner and exquisite personality, no money wealth can compare with its value.

This blessing is not difficult of acquisition, for a sunny face is but a reflection of a warm, generous heart. The sunshine does not appear first upon the face, but in the soul. The glad smile that makes the face radiant is but a glimpse of the soul's sunshine.

By taking a large-hearted interest in everyone we meet, by trying to pierce through the mask of the outer man or woman, to the inmost core, and by cultivating kindly feelings toward all, it is possible to acquire this inestimable gift. It is really only the development of our own finest qualities that enables us to understand and draw out what is fine and noble in others. Nothing will pay one better than the acquisition of the power to make others feel at ease, happy, and satisfied with themselves.

Sunny people dispel melancholy, gloom,

worry, and anxiety from all those with whom they come in contact, just as the sun drives away darkness. When they enter a roomful of people, where the conversation has been lagging, and where everybody seems bored, they transform the surroundings like the sun bursting through thick, black clouds after a storm. Everybody takes on a joyous spirit from the glad soul just entered, tongues are untied, conversation which dragged becomes bright and spirited, and the whole atmosphere vibrates with gladness and good cheer.

There is nothing which you could put into your life, except service to others, which would pay you so well as the cultivation of sunshine in your business or profession, and in your social relations. Business will come to you instead of having to be sought, friends will seek you, society open wide its doors to you. A cheerful disposition is a fund of ready capital, a magnet for the good things of life.

Force yourself, if necessary, to form the habit of seeing the best in people, of finding out their good qualities, and dwelling upon them and enlarging them. Do not see the distorted, crooked, cramped, burlesque of a man, but the man that God made. Ruskin says: " Do

CHEERFUL THINKING

not think of your faults; still less of others' faults. In every person who comes near you, look for what is good and strong. Honor that; rejoice in it; and as you can, try to imitate it, and your faults will drop off like dead leaves when their time comes."

If you make up your mind firmly that you will never again speak unkindly of any one, that if you cannot find anything good in them, if you cannot see the best side, you will see nothing and say nothing, it will make a wonderful difference in life for you. You will be surprised to see how soon everything will respond with a message of joy and peace. If you always look on the sunny side of every incident, you will find that there is really very little trouble in the world for you, and even that little can be turned to goodness. Your vinegary countenance and cynical remarks will be cast off as an ugly mask which has been hiding your real, wholesome, happy self, and all the blessings of human experience will be yours.

> *"Catch the sunshine! Don't be grieving*
> *O'er that darksome billow there!*
> *Life's a sea of stormy billows,*
> *We must meet them everywhere.*

Pass right through them! Do not tarry.
* Overcome the heaving tide,*
There's a sparkling gleam of sunshine
* Waiting on the other side."*

Talk happiness. The world is sad enough
Without your woe. No path is wholly rough.
Look for the places that are smooth and clear,
And speak of them to rest the weary ear
Of earth, so hurt by one continuous strain
Of mortal discontent and grief and pain.

—ELLA WHEELER WILCOX.

X. NEGATIVE CREEDS PARALYZE

X. NEGATIVE CREEDS PARALYZE

Denials should be ignored entirely, for they are but reminders of a condition we are trying to erase from the memory—and by verbal expression of any condition or fact we form a mental image thereof.—AGNES PROCTER.

NEGATIVES never accomplish anything. There is no life in a negative, nothing but deterioration, destruction, death. Negatives are great enemies of the success candidate. The man who is always talking down everything, who is always complaining of hard times and bad business, poor health and poverty, attracts to himself all the destructive, negative influences about him, and neutralizes all of his endeavor.

Constructive thought abandons the man who is always thinking destructively, and using destructive language, for he has nothing kindred with the positive, nothing to attract it. The creative principles cannot live in a negative, destructive atmosphere, and no signal achievement can take place there. So negative people are always on the down grade, always turning out failures. They lose the power of affirmation, and drift, unable to get ahead.

Negatives will paralyze your ambition, my young friend, if you indulge in them. They will poison your life. They will rob you of power. They will kill your self-confidence until you are a victim of your situation instead of a master of it. The power to do is largely a question of self-faith, self-confidence. No matter what you undertake, you will never do it until you think you can. You will never master it until you first feel the mastery and do the deed in your mind. It must be thought out or it can never be wrought out. It must be a mind accomplishment before it can be a material one.

There is no science in the world which will bring a thing to you while your thought repels it, while doubt and suspicion linger in the mind. No man can pass his self-imposed bounds or limitations. The man who would get up in the world must learn to deny his belief in limitation. He must throw all negative suggestions to the wind. He must think success before he can achieve it. He must affirm continually with decision and vigor that which he wishes to accomplish or be.

Suppose a boy some morning should say,

"I can't get up, I can't get up; what's the use of trying?" It is perfectly sure that he never could get out of bed until he thought he could, until he had confidence in his ability to get up.

How can a boy expect to rise in the world when he is all the time saying to himself: "I can't do this thing. It is useless to try, I know I can't do it. Other boys may do it, but I know I can't." The boy who thinks he can't get his lessons, who decides that he can't solve his problems, who is sure he can't go through college, can never do any of these things. Very soon he becomes the victim of chronic "can't." Negation has mastered him. "I can't" has become the habit of his life. All self-respect and self-confidence, all consciousness of ability, have been undermined and destroyed. His achievement cannot rise higher than his thoughts.

Contrast this with the boy who always says, "I will." No matter what obstacles confront him, he says, "I will do the thing I have undertaken." It is the constant affirmation of his determination to do the thing which increases his confidence in himself, and the power to do the thing, until he actually does it.

It would be impossible for a lawyer to make

a reputation in his profession while continually thinking about medicine or engineering. He must think about law, he must study and become thoroughly imbued with its principles. It is absolutely unscientific to expect to attain excellence or ability enough to gain distinction in any particular line while holding the mind open and continually contemplating something radically different. Is it not, therefore, more than foolish, even ridiculous, to expect to develop a strong, vigorous mentality, while acknowledging or contemplating weakness or deficiency?

As long as you contemplate any personal defect—mental, moral, or physical—you will fall below your possible attainment; you cannot approach your ideal, your standard.

As long as you allow negative, destructive, tearing-down processes to exist in your mind, you cannot create anything, and you will be a weakling.

Most people go through life crippled and handicapped by thinking weak thoughts, diseased thoughts, failure thoughts. It would be just as sensible for a girl to try to develop the highest type of beauty of physique and character by holding in her mind the ugliest ideals and thinking of herself as hideous. If she wishes to be beautiful, she must hold steadily the beauty ideal in her mind and try to measure up to it; then not only the physical but also the moral nature responds to this effort to attain the æsthetic ideal; but if she goes through life thinking she is ugly and deformed, and lamenting the fact, beauty will never respond.

What a misfortune to see bright young men or young women hampered and kept back in their careers because of holding the sickly ideal, the confession of weakness and defect. Banish these ghosts, these unrealities, these enemies of your success and happiness, forever from your mind. Rise up out of the valley of despair and despondency, out of the miasma which has poisoned the air around you, out of the foulness which has suffocated you all these years, into the atmosphere of excellence, of power, of beauty; then you will begin to accomplish something in life, to be somebody.

If people could only once realize the demoralizing influence of holding the sickly ideal, the failure ideal, in the mind until the standards of excellence are all dragged down to the level of mediocrity or commonness, they would never again be content to dwell in the valley of failure, to live in the basements of their lives.

How can a man be free, prosperous, and happy while he is imprisoned and enslaved by the poverty thought, the conviction that he is poor and unlucky, and that he can never accumulate money as others do?

In what condition is a man to fight for prosperity when he has lost confidence in his ability, and is convinced that opportunity is for others and not for him? He cannot make a strenuous, energetic effort to release himself from this condition while he holds this failure thought. He does not believe he can push away the limitations which hedge him in. He sees no way to regain his confidence and self-trust, to get a foothold. So he still thinks poverty, talks poverty, acts poverty, dreams poverty, and then wonders why he is unlucky.

He has made himself a negative magnet, he repels all the success qualities, and attracts only those of failure. He has lost his magnetic power to attract the forces which can extricate him from sickly, deadly environment.

How many people drag through weary years of self-imposed invalidism. They can never rise into the health atmosphere while they are contemplating the sickly ideal in the mind.

NEGATIVE CREEDS

Deep-rooted convictions of disease actually produce their physical counterparts.

The conviction, for example, that you have inherited the seeds of some terrible disease, such as cancer, and the fact that your physician has told you it is liable to show itself soon after the age of forty, keep you expectantly looking for the symptoms of this disease, and may develop an ordinary sore into an ulcer.

A young girl, delicate, sensitive to cold, has been told from her early childhood that she must exercise the greatest possible care because she has surely inherited a consumptive tendency from her mother, who died of consumption. This black picture of consumption and its fearful ravages in the system stamps itself indelibly upon the young life, and prevents healthful, buoyant growth or prompt physical reaction.

Dwelling upon these conditions ruins the appetite, disturbs digestion, cuts off the assimilation of food, until emaciation sets in as a result, and, as if this were not enough to discourage and dishearten the victim, everybody has to tell her how bad she looks, how she is growing thinner and thinner every day. Very often they say: "Now be careful, you know your mother went just by taking cold, by exposure to a draught." They stuff her with cod-liver oil and tonics, but these are sorry compensations for the resisting power of the mind, of which they have cruelly robbed her; a poor substitute for the God-given power of self-protection, granted to every human being. They have disturbed the child's beautiful natural feeling that it is protected by the Almighty arm, that it is made in God's image, and hence God-defended, and that nothing can injure its reality. Many a beautiful life has been stifled by such inculcated fears and depressing influences.

What a pitiable sight to see a large proportion of the human race dogged through life by such hideous pictures, dragging this terrible load of expectation of being run down, overcome, crushed by some cruel fate, attacked by some awful disease, the consequences of the sins of our ancestors. This would be like sending a boy to prison or to the gallows because his father committed robbery or murder. The sooner we get this damnable philosophy out of the minds of the young, the better for the world. It would be just as reasonable to say that the sun casts shadows, that love radiates hatred, that harmony carries hidden discord in its very nature. To hold such beliefs is not only cruelly wicked, but also absurd. The Creator does not blight our lives and prospects in this way. These fearsome pictures are drawn by human artists; they have no divine origin. No matter what the conditions of our birth, we have the power of the Infinite to overcome them.

XI. AFFIRMATION CREATES POWER

XI. AFFIRMATION CREATES POWER

"An affirmation is a statement of Truth consciously used so as to become the directing power of Life's expression."

ONLY he can who thinks he can! The world makes way only for the determined man, for the man who laughs at barriers which limit others, at stumbling-blocks over which others fall. The man who, as Emerson says, "hitches his wagon to a star," is more likely to arrive at his goal than the one who trails in the slimy path of the snail.

Confidence is the father of achievement. It reënforces ability, doubles energy, buttresses mental faculties, increases power.

Your thought will carry only the force of your conviction, the weight of your decision, the power of your confidence. If these are weak, your thought will be weak and your work futile. Some people are incapable of strong, deep conviction; they are all surface, and liable to be changed by the opinions of everybody else. If they resolve upon a certain course, their resolution is so superficial that the first obstacle they strike deflects them. They are always at the mercy of the opposition, or of people who do not agree with them. Such people are shifty and unreliable; they lack strength of decision, positiveness of resolution.

What is a man good for if he hasn't strength of resolution? If his convictions are on the surface, he stands for nothing; nobody has confidence in him. He may be a good man, personally, but he does not inspire confidence. No one would think of calling upon him when anything of importance was at stake. Unless conviction takes hold of one's very being, there will be very little achievement in life. It is the man whose conviction is rooted deep and takes hold of his very life-blood, the man who is strong and persistent in his determination, that can be depended upon. He is the man of influence, who carries weight; he is above the influence of any man who happens to have a different opinion.

If young people only knew the power of affirmation, of the habit of holding in the mind persistently and affirming that they are what they wish to be, that they can do what they have attempted, it would revolutionize their whole lives, it would exempt them from most of their ills and troubles, and carry them to heights of which they scarcely dream.

We are always talking about the power of the will. Its exercise is only another form of affirmation. The will, the determination to do a thing, is the same as the affirmation of the ability to do it. No one ever accomplishes anything in this world until he affirms in one way or another that he can do what he undertakes. It is almost impossible to keep a man back who has a firm faith in his mission, who believes that he can do the thing before him, that he is equal to the obstacles which confront him, that he is more than a match for his environment. The constant affirmation of ability to succeed, and of our determination to do so, carries us past difficulties, defies obstacles, laughs at misfortunes, and strengthens the power to achieve. It reënforces and buttresses the natural faculties and powers, and holds them to their tasks.

Constant affirmation increases courage, and courage is the backbone of confidence. Furthermore, when a person gets in a tight place and says " I must," " I can," " I will," he not only reënforces his courage and strengthens his confidence, but also weakens the opposite qualities. Whatever strengthens a positive will weaken the corresponding negative.

You can do a difficult thing only with a positive state of mind, never with a negative. Plus force, not minus, does things. The dominant qualities are all positive, assertive, aggressive, and they require a corresponding attitude of mind for their exercise and application. A man who has not these dominant qualities can never be a leader or independent; he must be a trailer, an imitator, until he changes his thought from negative to positive, from doubtful to certain, from shrinking and retiring to asserting and advancing. It is the decisive, positive soul that wins.

If you wish to amount to anything in the world, never for one moment permit the idea to come into your mind that you are unlucky, that you are less fortunate than other human beings. Deny it with all the power you can muster. Discipline yourself never to acknowledge weakness or think of mental, physical, or moral defects. Deny that you are a weakling, that you cannot do what others can do; that you are handicapped and must be satisfied to take an inferior position in the world. Strangle every doubt as you would a viper threatening your life. Never talk, think, or write of your poverty or unfortunate condition. Cut out of your life all thought that limits, hampers, dwarfs, and darkens it. These are ghosts of fear; the Creator never made them or intended them to haunt and torment you. He made you for happiness, for joy, for conquest over your environment.

Persistently affirm that the Creator handicapped no one; that our limitations are all our own. Resolve that, come what may, you will be an optimist; that there shall be nothing pessimistic in you; believe in the final triumph of the right, the victory of all that is true and noble. Affirm that you are one of the most fortunate beings. Congratulate yourself that you were born just in the nick of time, and in just the right place; that there is a definite work for you to do that no one else can do; and that you are one of the most lucky persons in the world to have the opportunity, the health, the education, to do the thing you are bound to accomplish.

If you are out of work and poor, just throw out of your mind every idea of penury and poverty. Hold the thought of plenty, of abundance, of all good, which the Creator has promised you. Stoutly deny that you are poor, or miserable, or unlucky; claim that you are lucky, that you are well, vigorous, and strong; that you must succeed; and you will succeed. Always affirm that the Creator who gave you the longing to be somebody and to do something in the world, has also given you the ability and the opportunity to realize the ambition.

When you set your mind toward achievement, let everything about you indicate success. Let your manner, your dress, your bearing, your conversation, and everything you do speak achievement and success. Carry always a success atmosphere with you.

You will find a wonderful advantage in starting out every morning with the mind set toward success and achievement by permeating it with thoughts of prosperity and harmony, whether by repetition of set formulas, as some advise, or not. It will then be so much the harder for discord to get into the day's work. If you are inclined to doubt your ability to do any particular thing, school yourself to hold the self-trust thought firmly and persistently. It is the assumption of power, of self-trust, of confidence in yourself, in your integrity or wholeness, that cannot be shaken, that will enable you to become strong, and to do, with vigor and ease, the thing you undertake.

AFFIRMATION

You will find that the perpetual holding of these ideals will change your whole outlook upon life. You will approach your problems from a new standpoint, and life will take on a fresh meaning. This perpetual affirmation will put you in harmony with your surroundings; it will make you contented and happy; and it will be a powerful tonic for your health. It will help you to build up individuality and personal power. It will make your brain clearer, your thought more effective. Keeping the mental machinery clean makes for vigorous thinking, decisive action.

If you are deficient in any quality, you can strengthen it by constant affirmation. If you are a coward anywhere in your nature (and most people are), you can strengthen courage by constantly affirming that you are absolutely fearless, that you are courageous, that nothing can harm you. Reason that fear is simply the sense of danger, and when you have perfect confidence in the great Creator's purpose, when you trust it implicitly, there will be no cause for fear. If you have convinced yourself that there is only one great cause, that the opposite must be a delusion, you will gradually lose the sense of fear and gain the courage you desire.

Every time you feel a sense of fear come over you say: " I am absolutely fearless; there is nothing to fear; fear is not a reality; it is not the truth of being. It is only the absence of courage, based upon ignorance of the great cause." Emerson knew the virtue of this philosophy when he said: " Nerve us with incessant affirmation. Don't bark against the bad, but chant the beauties of the good."

Stoutly determine not to harbor anything in the mind which you do not wish to become real in your life. Shun poisoned thoughts, ideas which depress and make you unhappy, as instinctively as you avoid physical danger of any kind. Do not entertain a discordant or an unhappy thought, or a thought of weakness and misery, but replace all these with cheerful, hopeful, optimistic thoughts. When you feel out of sorts, blue, discouraged, disheartened, if you form the habit of suggesting to yourself some agreeable or pleasant subject, to dwell upon or think about, or take up some word or idea which will suggest pleasure, happiness, and harmony, you will be surprised to see how quickly you can change the whole course of your thought, and when this is changed, the feeling will change also. You will increase your courage and confidence, and this is half the battle. You will soon find that your environment will begin to change. Hope will brighten, you will have a healthier outlook upon life. Then thought, instead of depressing your mind, will be a perpetual tonic of encouragement, and light will soon break and drive out the darkness.

All that you dream of, all that you yearn for and long to be, will be within your reach if you have the power to affirm sufficiently strong, if you can focus your faculties with sufficient intentness on a single purpose. It is concentration upon the thing you wish that brings it to you, whether it is health, money, or position. Constantly affirm that which you wish, hold it persistently in the thought, concentrate all the power of your mind upon it, and when the mind is sufficiently positive and creative the desired thing will come to you as certainly as a stone will come to the earth, when left free in the air, through the attracting influence of gravitation. You make yourself a magnet to draw the condition you wish.

XII. THOUGHTS RADIATE AS INFLUENCE

XII. THOUGHTS RADIATE AS INFLUENCE

Gaze thou in the face of thy brother, in those eyes where plays the lambent fire of kindness, or in those where rages the lurid conflagration of anger; feel how thy own so quiet soul is straightway involuntarily kindled with the like, and ye blaze and reverberate on each other, till it is all one limitless, confluent flame (of embracing love, or of deadly, grasping hate); and then say what miraculous virtue goes out of man into man.—CARLYLE.

OUR thoughts, while most powerfully acting on our own lives, by no means exhaust their force there. They are not held prisoners within our minds or bodies. Potent with influence, they fly from us every instant, working for weal or for woe.

"Every thought which genius and piety throw into the world alters the world," says Emerson. This must not be taken merely to mean printed thoughts, or thoughts spoken from pulpit or rostrum, or even thoughts spoken at all. Our most secret, unuttered thoughts go forth and affect the world, the people all about us.

Every man has an atmosphere peculiar to

himself, pervaded by all of his characteristics, his ambitions and aspirations, absolutely determined by the thoughts that govern all his actions. The impression which he gives everybody who comes in contact with him partakes of his ideal. The quality of his ambition enters into his every voluntary act.

It is not what you say so much as the bearing of your thought toward others that forms their estimate of you. Do not flatter yourself that you are known only by what you say; that you are measured by what you choose to give people about yourself. You create in others the impression which you hold in your own mind. What you think about modifies and reaffirms others' opinions of you. They feel the quality of your thought, they know whether it has power or weakness, whether it is clean, lofty, and noble, or base and low. They can tell by your silent radiations the character of your ideals, and they estimate you accordingly. In fact, this conviction which has come from their silent impression of you may be held firmly, even against your verbal protest to the contrary. As Emerson says, " What you are speaks so loud, I cannot hear what you say." The atmosphere we radiate must, of necessity, partake of ourselves.

We cannot radiate anything unlike ourselves. It does not matter what we pretend to be. People who know us take our real measure, not the pretended one.

We can best estimate the effect we produce on others by analyzing the effect other persons have upon us. We know our real friends by the bearing of their thought toward us. We know that they feel generous and magnanimous toward us, whatever our faults. They are constantly radiating themselves into our consciousness.

It does not matter how pleasant, agreeable, or considerate a man may be toward us, if he holds antagonistic thoughts, mean thoughts, if he carries a grudge, if he is not what he pretends to be, our instinct will penetrate beneath his pretence and unmask his real self, and while he thinks he deceives us, we feel instinctively what he really is.

How often one hears "I can't bear that man; he gives me the creeps." Yet the individual in question may have been doing his best to make a good impression, and thinking all the time that he was succeeding.

In the home and in the office, in every relation of life, radiation of one's own thoughts plays an important part. No care and effort can be too great that make this radiating influence always helpful, uplifting, beneficent.

How much harm we can do in a single day by casting a dark shadow across some bright life, depressing buoyancy, crushing hopes, strangling aspirations—more harm than we can undo in years. We should be appalled if we could see pass before us in vivid panorama the wrecks of a lifetime, caused by cruel thought. A stab here, a thrust there, a cruel, malicious sarcasm, bitter irony, ungenerous criticisms, jealous thought, envious thought, hatred, anger, revengeful thought are all going out constantly from many a mind on their deadly missions.

A morose, gloomy, crestfallen mortal flings out his pessimism wherever he goes and poisons the atmosphere around him, surcharging it with heaviness, depression, and sadness. Success and happiness are not born in such an atmosphere. Hope cannot live in it; joy flees from it. No child can be happy in it. Laughter is suppressed; sweet, joyous faces become cloudy. We feel that life would be unendurable if we had to remain in it indefinitely. What a relief it is when such a person drags his depressing presence from us.

Some people make us feel mean and contemptible in their presence. They call out of us meanness which we never knew we possessed and make us almost despise ourselves. Marriage sometimes reveals undesirable qualities which neither husband nor wife suspected in themselves before.

Some people emit a sort of miasmatic atmosphere, which poisons everything that comes within its reach. No matter how generous and magnanimous we felt before, when these characters come near us we shrivel and shrink within ourselves and there is no responsiveness, no spontaneity possible until they go out of our presence. Like disturbed clams, we shut ourselves up as tightly as possible until we feel that we are out of danger. We cannot be ourselves when near such people. We try to be agreeable with them, but somehow everything is forced; we cannot be sociable with them. We seem ill at ease until they have departed; then we feel that a heavy weight is lifted from us, and we are ourselves again.

Other people act like a tonic or an invigorating and refreshing breeze. They make us feel like new beings. By the inspiration of their presence they stimulate our thoughts, quicken our faculties, sharpen our intellect, open the flood-gates of language and sentiment, and awaken the poetic within us.

These diverse effects come from the radiation or expression of personality, and we ourselves are producing such on others all the time. We radiate what we feel and believe, our fleeting moods and our deep-seated convictions. What we think most about and strive to become, we radiate to others in our every letter, in every conversation, in our manner, in our life. Spirit is contagious, and will be quickly perceived or even taken on by those with whom we come in contact. If the mind is in harmony and peace, if it is strong and healthy, we radiate health, peace, and harmony wherever we go.

On the contrary, if you are in doubt, if you are discouraged and disheartened, you will communicate discouraged thoughts. How can a mind always filled with self-depreciation, distrust, and the dread of failure radiate the confidence which is necessary to insure credit and assistance from others? If you hold mean, contemptible thoughts, if you harbor revenge, jealousy, and envy, you reflect these thoughts to those about you.

If you are selfish, you cannot help radiating the selfish thought. Everybody about you

THOUGHTS

will feel your meanness, and will measure you accordingly.

If you are a miser, if you are greedy and avaricious, you cannot get away from your greed, but you must pay the penalty of your aim. You cannot radiate magnanimity, if you are mean and stingy. If the attitude of your mind dwarfs and stunts all that is beautiful in life, if the tendency of your mind is to hinder, you cannot give out the opposite to the world. If you think blighting, chilling thoughts, you will radiate the same. Your aspirations and longings, whether for money or for fame, or real helpfulness to others, will determine the character of your radiations.

As we can only communicate the quality of our thought at the moment, how important that we control these thoughts, and make them clean, pure, true thoughts, instead of foul, demoralizing, doubtful ones.

Servants have actually been made dishonest by other persons perpetually holding the suspicion that they were dishonest. This thought continually held by people who are naturally suspicious, suggests the thought perhaps to the suspected for the first time, and being constantly held there takes root and grows, and bears the fruit of theft.

It is simply cruel to hold a suspicious thought of another until you have positively proved its authenticity. That other person's mind is sacred; you have no right to invade it with your miserable thoughts and pictures of suspicion. You should keep your wicked thoughts at home; but, as this is impossible, you should not harbor them, any more than you would allow yourself to hold thoughts of sin or crime. Many a being has been made wretched and miserable for years, depressed, despondent, and borne down by the uncharitable, wicked thoughts of those about them.

Many people scatter fear thoughts, doubt thoughts, failure thoughts, wherever they go; and these take root in minds that might otherwise be free from them and therefore happy, confident, and successful.

Be sure that when you hold an evil thought toward another, an unhealthy thought, a discordant thought, a disease thought, a deadly thought, something is wrong in your mind. You should call, "Halt! about face!" Look toward the sunlight; determine that, if you cannot do any good in the world, you will not scatter seeds of poison, the venom of malice and hatred.

Always hold kindly thoughts, charitable,

magnanimous, loving thoughts toward everybody; then you will not depress them, and hinder them, but will scatter sunshine and gladness instead of sadness and shadow, help and encouragement instead of discouragement.

Be one of those who are always radiating success thoughts, health thoughts, joy thoughts, uplifting, helpful thoughts, scattering sunshine wherever they go. These are the helpers of the world, the lighteners of burdens, the people who ease the jolts of life and soothe the wounded and give solace to the discouraged.

Learn to radiate joy, not stingily, not meanly, but generously. Fling out your gladness without reserve. Shed it in the home, on the street, on the car, in the store, everywhere, as the rose sheds its beauty and flings out its fragrance.

When the world learns that love thoughts heal—that they carry balm to wounds; that thoughts of harmony, of beauty, and of truth always uplift, beautify, and ennoble; that the opposite carry death, destruction, and blight everywhere—it will learn the true secret of right living.

XIII. HOW THINKING BRINGS SUCCESS

XIII. HOW THINKING BRINGS SUCCESS

He who dares assert the I,
May calmly wait
While hurrying fate
Meets his demands with sure supply.

—HELEN WILMANS.

A STRONG man hypnotized into a belief that he cannot rise from his chair is actually powerless to do so till the spell is removed. A frail woman, nerved by necessity for saving life, can carry a person heavier than herself from danger by fire or flood. In both cases the mental attitude, not the physical ability, determines the result, yet both acts are only work for muscle. When a task to be done consists largely or wholly of mental acts, as do most kinds of success winning, how much greater must be the determining power of the thought and mental attitude! The conquerors of the world, whether on battlefields, in trade, or in moral struggles, have won by the attitude of mind in which they went at the work they had to do.

I wish it were possible to impress upon the

minds of the young the tremendous power which right thinking has to bring about success. Realization of our inherent capacity for great things, conviction that we are intended to succeed, and that it is a positive sin to spoil the plans of our Creator by failing, would revolutionize our lives and abolish most of our ills and troubles.

The belief in limitations, the conviction that we cannot rise out of our environments, that we are the victims of circumstances, is responsible for a weakening of achievement faculties and an undermining of executive ability which cause untold tragic failures, a large part of the poverty and wretchedness of mankind. Such belief is abnormal, and it produces abnormal conditions. Dominion was man's birthright, but he has adopted weakness and limitation. He has claimed poverty, wretchedness, and slavery in place of riches, happiness, and freedom, and how can a man rise out of his wretchedness until he thinks and believes he can? Is there any science whereby a man can, when he thinks he can't? Is there any philosophy whereby a man can rise, until he looks up? Is there any way by which a man can succeed while he thinks, talks, and lives a failure? Man cannot go in opposite directions at the

THINKING BRINGS SUCCESS

same time; there is no certainty in the presence of doubt. Until you erase "fate" and "can't" and "doubt" from your vocabulary, you cannot rise. You cannot get strong while you harbor convictions of your weakness, or be happy while you dwell on your miseries or misfortunes.

A person might as well expect to become healthy and strong by always thinking and talking about his poor health, saying that he never expects to be robust, as to expect the executive faculties to be strong and vigorous while he is perpetually doubting his ability to do what he undertakes. Nothing so weakens the mind and renders it totally unfit for effective thinking as the constant acknowledgment of weakness, or doubt of one's ability to accomplish.

The majority of persons who fail begin by doubting their ability to do the things they attempt. The moment a young man starting out on a career admits doubt into his mind, he is letting an enemy into his camp, a spy who will betray him. Doubt belongs to the failure family, and once admitted and not expelled will introduce "Mr. Take-it-Easy," "Mr. Let-up-a-Little," "Mr. Let-Go-When-It-Gets-Hard," "Mr. Wait," and other members of the failure family. When these once get into the mind, they attract other qualities like themselves, and there is an end of ambition. Your longing for prosperity and yearning for achievement will all be vain while you are entertaining the idlers, the losers, the failures. They will exhaust your energy, destroy your power for attracting success. Failure will soon be in the ascendancy in your mind and in your actions.

The moment you admit weakness, the moment you confess defeat, you are gone. There is no hope for a man who has lost his stamina, who has given up the struggle; you can't do anything with him. If there is anything despicable in the world, it is a human being who has lain down, who has given up, who says " I can't," " It's no use," " The world's against me," " I am down on my luck." To hold perpetually the thought that you are down, that you cannot rise, that success is for others, but not for you, is to adjust yourself to your thought, and to make any other condition impossible. How can you expect to be lucky when you are always talking about your ill luck? As long as you think you are a poor miserable worm of the dust you will be that. You cannot rise above your thought; you cannot be different from your conception of yourself. If you really believe you are unhappy, unlucky, and miserable, you will be so. There are no drugs, or patent medicines, or influences in the world that can get you out of this condition until you change your thought; and a reversal of thought will bring about a reversal of conditions in the body, as surely as the sun and the rain unfold the petals of a rosebud. There is no mystery about it; it is purely scientific.

People who do great things are powerful in their affirmations. They have tremendous positive ability; they do not know the meaning of negatives. Their power of assertion and their conviction of ability to do are so strong that the opposites do not trouble them. When they make up their minds to do a thing, they take it for granted that they can do it. They are not filled with doubts and fears, no matter how people may scoff, and cry "Crank." In fact nearly all the great men and women who have pushed progress along have been called cranks. The world said they had "wheels in their heads." We owe the blessings of modern civilization to the sublime confidence of such men and women in themselves, that indomitable faith in their mission which nothing could shake. The history of all great forward movements is contained in their biographies.

What if Copernicus and Galileo had given up when they were denounced as cranks and insane? Science of to-day is built on their unshaken confidence that the world is round and that the earth moves around the sun instead of the sun around it! Suppose Columbus had given up and lost confidence in himself when Europe was laughing at him as a crank! Suppose Cyrus W. Field had lain down after a dozen years of fruitless endeavor to span the sea, when cable after cable had parted in mid-ocean! Suppose he had listened to his relatives, who said he was wasting his fortune, and would die in poverty! Suppose Fulton had given up under ridicule when a book was written to prove that a ship could not carry coal enough to force its way across the ocean! He lived to see that very book brought across the sea in a steamship. What if Alexander Graham Bell had lost faith in himself when he had expended his last dollar in experimenting on the principle of the telephone, and when the world called him a crank?

When Savonarola entered Florence as a poor, obscure priest, and saw the abject misery on every hand—brought about by unreasonable luxury and fawning on wealth—he immediately determined that he would uplift the standard of living. Although constantly approached with bribes, money never influenced him. He kept his ideal always in sight. He found Lorenzo di Medici at the height of his power. At that time the worldly Alexander VI., who sympathized with the wealthy and the powerful, was at the head of the papacy. This did not discourage the sanguine reformer, and, fighting almost single-handed against overwhelming odds, believing that justice would triumph, he finally did succeed in overthrowing the Medici despotism, and established what he desired, a state " wherein justice shall rule." Savonarola died a martyr to the Church, lifting its ideal high above the commonplace by helping to bring about the Protestant reformation.

When Wolfe was called before a committee of Parliament and told that he had been selected to lead the British in Canada, he was asked if he thought he could end the war. He brandished his sword about the room, struck the table with it, and exhibited such extreme vainglory and egotism that the committee was disgusted, and regretted its choice. But when young Wolfe was leading his forces up to the Plains of Abraham, this same confidence enabled him to vanquish the French forces under Montcalm.

Napoleon, Bismarck, Hugo, and many other great men have had such colossal faith in themselves that they have excited antagonism and even ridicule, but this quality is essential to all great achievement. It has doubled, trebled, quadrupled, the ordinary power of these men. How else can we account for the achievement of a Luther, a Wesley, a Savonarola? Without this sublime faith, this confidence in her mission, how could the fragile village maiden, Jeanne Darc, have led and controlled a French army? Without this power how could she have led those thousands of stalwart men as if they were children? This divine confidence multiplied her power a thousandfold, until even the king obeyed her.

When our nation was threatened with civil war, the apparently modest and unassuming Lincoln told some politicians that if they would nominate him for President, he could be elected, and that he could run the Government. Think of this self-confidence of a man born in a log cabin, with almost no advantages of education or culture. Think of the sublime self-confidence of Grant—who two years before had been an obscure merchant, almost unknown outside of his own little community—when he told Lincoln that he could end the Civil War. He did end it, in spite of as severe public condemnation as a man ever received. Where would the United States be to-day had Lincoln and Grant lost confidence in themselves when denounced by the press?

The generals who had preceded Grant never had unreserved faith in their ability, as he had in his. Grant was the complete master of the situation because there was no interrogation point in his self-confidence. He knew he could conquer the enemy, if only he had the men and the opportunity. The others, always more or less in doubt, won only partial victories.

It was this grand self-confidence and faith in a just cause that led Jackson, with a handful of men, to administer a most crushing defeat to an army of trained English soldiers at New Orleans. It was such faith that enabled General Taylor at Buena Vista, with 5,000 American soldiers, to defeat Santa Anna, who had 20,000 men.

Confidence, absolute trust, is a creative force which generates, produces, and achieves, while distrust tears down, annihilates, and destroys.

A strong self-faith, by eliminating doubt and uncertainty, wonderfully increases the power of concentration, because it withdraws distracting motives. It makes possible a steady pushing forward, with no side-pulls and scattering energy.

Discoverers, inventors, reformers, generals, all have this spirit of invincible affirmation, while if we analyze failures we shall find that most of them are weak in their self-faith, that they lack the abounding confidence in themselves that marks successful persons. We cannot read the sealed orders which the Creator has placed in the hands of those destined to do great things, but the fact that one has an unconquerable faith in himself is pretty good evidence of his ability to do what he believes he can. The Creator does not mock us with such convictions of possibilities without granting the ability to do the deed.

Never allow yourself or any one else to shake your confidence in yourself, to destroy your self-reliance, for this is the very foundation of all great achievement. When that is gone, your whole structure falls; as long as you have it, there is hope for you. Confidence, unbounded, unshaken faith in yourself, which even amounts to boldness at times, is absolutely necessary in all great undertakings.

Self-faith helps inferior men to accomplish results by eliminating fear, doubt, and uncertainty, the great enemies of most men's achievement. The mind cannot act with vigor in the presence of doubt. Wavering in the mind makes wavering execution. There must be certainty, or there is no efficiency. The ignorant man who believes in himself, who has the faith that he can do the thing he undertakes, often puts to shame the college-bred man whose overculture and wider outlook have brought with increased sensitiveness a lessening of self-confidence, and whose decision is weakened by constant weighing of conflicting theories, whose prejudices are always open to conviction.

The ignorant man with great self-confidence, strong, vigorous self-assertion, lacks the finer sentiments, but is spared the finer suffering of a more sensitive, cultured mind. His brain powers have not been weakened by theories or by the knowledge of how much he does not know. He simply plunges ahead where a cultured man would hesitate.

The weakening of self-confidence, the development of timidity, is often an unfortunate result of a liberal education. I have known boys to enter college with unbounded confidence in what they could accomplish, with strong powers of self-assertion, who have been graduated with those qualities almost eliminated. They have been replaced by the gradual development of timidity, and a shrinking from positive statement of fact which seriously crippled the men's executive faculties.

Great scholars are proverbially retiring, shrinking, timid natures, often lacking almost entirely the executive faculty. Their self-assertion has disappeared, giving place to self-effacement. Unassuming humbleness, patience, and tolerance are very desirable qualities in their right places, but very unfortunate when they are not subordinated to vigorous self-faith and an aggressive self-assertion. These lovable qualities make the scholar more companionable, but less practical and less successful. The aggressive, executive faculties should be preserved intact at all hazards, or the career will be cramped and limited.

XIV. POWER OF SELF-FAITH OVER OTHERS

XIV. POWER OF SELF-FAITH OVER OTHERS

You conquer Fate by thought. If you think the fatal thought of men and institutions, you need never pull the trigger. The consequences of thinking inevitably follow.—CARLYLE.

UCCESS is not dependent solely on our earnest affirmation, on our self-confidence, but also on the confidence of others in us; but this confidence is very largely a reflection of our own, the effect of our own personality on them. Our own attitude of mind is therefore the means to produce this confidence in others. Your earnest affirmation is contagious. It affects every one with whom you come in contact, especially those whom you must master, whether as a teacher, as an orator, as an attorney, as salesman, as merchant, as possible employee, or in some other way. There is something that seems almost magical in the way a confident air influences other people. If you adopt or acquire it, you will be surprised to see how soon it will radiate to others, increasing their confidence in your

ability to do the thing you undertake. This is what makes reputation and establishes credit.

The men who possess conviction of ability to accomplish what they undertake are positive, strong characters. When a man feels a sense of mastery, of having risen to his dominion, he talks confidence, he radiates faith and conviction, and overcomes doubts in others, who catch the contagion of his constant affirmation of assurance and confidence, and believe this to be proof of ability to succeed. People believe in the man with a programme, the man who knows what he wants, who does not waver, but does things. Everything seems to stand aside for him. People who would oppose a man with weak self-confidence readily fall into line with his plans. Things which would trip and dishearten a man with little self-faith seem to favor the confident man's progress. It is human nature to help a man along the way he is going; if he is going up, the world will boost him; if he is going down, the world will kick him. If a man lacks faith in himself, the world will lack faith in him also.

We cannot help admiring a man who believes in himself. He cannot be laughed down, talked down, or written down. Poverty cannot dishearten him; misfortune deter him; hardship turn him a hair's breadth from his course. Whatever comes, he keeps his eye to the goal and pushes on. A determined face and an iron will win half the battles before a blow is struck. The writer knows a man who pushes everything he undertakes to completion, and has been remarkably successful because he never hesitates, he never has any doubt of his ability to do a thing. His self-faith, amounting to egotism at times, repels some people, but even they give way before him. While other people of finer texture or make-up are discussing the possibility or feasibility of doing something, doubting and wavering, this man does it. Such a man compels his opponents to believe in his ability in spite of real reasons against such faith. Average ability, coupled with such aggressive self-confidence, cuts a larger figure in the world, and gets more done, than superlative ability with the timid and shrinking nature that often goes with it. A teacher with a smattering of learning often succeeds better than one ten times as learned, but unable to pass it on to others or assert his mastery of the subject. This is not poetic justice, and often seems very unjust, but it is the actual state of affairs, and the remedy is for the really able to cultivate and assume the conviction that will impress other people.

In every kind of work and business we are dependent on the belief of others that we can make or carry out plans, can produce superior goods, can manage employees, can do any of the thousand things demanded by employers or by the public. Life is too short and the world too busy to allow minute investigation of another's ability to achieve the thing he professes to be able to do; therefore the world accepts, very largely, a man's own estimate of himself until he forfeits its confidence. If a young man hangs out his law shingle, the world will take it for granted that he is a lawyer, that he is fitted for his profession, until he proves otherwise. A physician does not have to prove to each patient that he has followed certain courses and passed certain examinations.

Therefore to acknowledge any inability, to give way to a temporary doubt, is to give failure so much advantage. We never should allow our self-faith to waver for a moment, no matter how dark the way may seem. Nothing will destroy confidence of others so quickly as doubt in our own minds, which those about us will soon feel. Many people fail because they radiate their discouraged moods, and project them into the minds of those about them.

If you are an employer, your employees can easily tell whether you come to your day's work as a conqueror, with a sense of victory, of confidence, or as a beaten man, in doubt and despair. They can tell whether you are going to win or lose during the day by your countenance, your manner.

In no business is the imparting of one's own confidence more potent than in salesmanship, whether it be in the agent, the commercial traveller, or the store clerk.

In all these kinds of selling, a species of hypnotism, of mental influence, is practised by great salesmen. An undecided customer—and most customers are hesitating between two opinions—can be brought to a decision by a skilful statement of the salesman's opinion, by narrowing down the articles considered from several to two, by an assumption that the decision is made and a move to cut off the goods or wrap up the article, in any one of a hundred ways that every good salesman practises continually. But with all these " tricks of the trade " must go the firm, decided, confident manner of the salesman, which is communicated to the purchaser. If a travelling agent lets doubt of a sale manifest itself in the slightest degree, the purchaser jumps at the chance to escape, and, after that, argument and persuasion are often useless.

No one has need of radiating proper mental attitudes more than the teacher. A flustered, worried, uncertain teacher will throw a whole roomful of children into disorder, when a calm, self-possessed, even-tempered person could have secured quiet and good work from the same set of pupils. A teacher must often overcome personal antagonism, harmonize quarrels between pupils, soothe worried little brains, too self-conscious to learn or recite, and impress knotty points of knowledge on minds that are too often inattentive. All this he does by personality, which is simply the radiation of one's own individuality. Young people are very susceptible to the character of the thought which is held toward them; they know whether the teacher is really interested in them and wants to help them or not. They are quick to feel selfish and unsympathetic natures. No teacher is fitted for his or her sacred task who is not naturally sympathetic, who does not hold loving, helpful thoughts toward pupils.

XV. BUILDING CHARACTER

XV. BUILDING CHARACTER

The universal self-delusion is this: when a man has a good thought, he fancies he has become what he thinks for the moment. Good thoughts are very good; but, unaccompanied by the difficult processes of character, they are often no better than soap-bubbles.
—MOZOOMDAR.

HOW strange that a young woman will spend many hours a day, for years, practising on a piano or training her voice, that a young man will give years of hard, dry study to the mastering of a profession or occupation, that an artist will spend half a lifetime in learning how to paint a picture, that an author will devote years to the production of one book, and yet be unwilling to spend any considerable time in building a character that will insure absolute peace of mind, contentment, and happiness under all circumstances! How pitiable it is to see a man sacrifice the best years of his life to scraping together a few thousand or a few million dollars! Working early and late, he has never thought it worth while to devote even a few minutes each day to building up a

wholesome, symmetrical, contented character, to acquiring something which would protect him and insure his serenity and self-poise no matter what losses and misfortunes might overtake him.

Most of us seem to think that that which is worth more than all else should come without effort, without special training or drill. In the case of a few individuals of fortunate heredity and advantageous environment this may occur, but most of us need some active and intelligent direction or effort. As Herbert Spencer said: " By no political alchemy can we get golden conduct out of leaden instincts. But instincts can be changed; fresh grafts can be introduced upon the stock; the whole tree can be trained in a new direction, and so golden conduct be made to flow from a golden character."

How easy it is to train the tender shoot in any direction, to make it assume any shape we wish, when it first comes up through the soil! And how much this training means to the symmetry and beauty of the future tree. How easy for the mother, if she but know how to train the young mind, to turn it from all its little enemies, all the fear thoughts, and worry thoughts, the despondent thoughts, the sick thoughts, the failure thoughts, as well as from the more vicious and recognizedly immoral thoughts!

In the past, much of the effort to build up character has been dwelling on faults. Parents have reminded their children, a hundred times a day, of some defect, until the poor children have had that failing constantly in mind with the fixed idea that it was branded into their natures, and that it was not of much use to try to be different. This way of trying to build up character is a good deal like trying to attain success by thinking all the time of failure. Continual thinking about defects in character, one's sins and faults, will impress them and make them harder to eradicate. We gradually become negative to good qualities by dwelling upon destructive characteristics. By reading continually of diseases, medical students often experience symptoms of those diseases, and sometimes the maladies themselves. Similarly, by dwelling on desirable qualities we may acquire success or happiness. It is by " fresh grafts " and suggestions of the virtues that the soundest character growth is secured.

A little care in choosing a child's vocabulary, in teaching it that words are real things, and that they imprint on the mind the images they call up, will make all the difference between happiness and misery, success and failure. How easy it is to help the child select those words which convey pictures of life and joy, light and peace, comfort and happiness; to banish those discordant, jarring words which contaminate the mind by the images they stamp there, and which ultimately ruin the character and destroy the life.

Plays are now introduced into kindergarten schools which tend to develop and awaken the desired qualities which are perhaps lacking in the children. "Justice plays," for example, or "courage plays" exercise certain functions and character qualities and are known to influence the pupils wonderfully. The constant repetition of "good manners plays" arouses, for instance, a spirit of gallantry and a sense of etiquette in a boy until he unconsciously takes off his hat in the presence of a lady without thinking of it.

The ideal home is a perpetual training school where children are always practising courage plays, courtesy plays, helpfulness plays, charity plays, plays of honesty and truthfulness; and what is at first simulated becomes natural, producing sweetness, beauty, and strength of character. Qualities apparently deficient can be awakened and developed in a marvellous degree in the young. So it is now believed that it is possible to develop strong character even in the average child under continuous, proper, scientific training. These repeated thought acts develop corresponding brain cells until they respond at the slightest suggestion from an affinity—the same as the brain spontaneously responds with the correct result when we think of adding or subtracting figures. At first the suggestion had to be made and the thought repeated many times, but after a while the repetition became automatic in the brain, and we performed abstruse mathematical problems while scarcely thinking of the processes; so we train the mind to the character qualities which we desire.

It is simply a question of holding the thought persistently toward the thing we desire until the new brain structure develops by exercise, becomes dominant, then the character is set and will act automatically, and the law "to him that hath, more shall be given," and the reverse, comes into play.

It has been found that manual training, learning to use the hands ingeniously, has its influence upon the brain, and develops deficient faculties to a remarkable degree. A boy who is naturally lazy and indolent, whose faculties for doing things seem to be wholly deficient, can be so trained in a short time that he will love to work. As soon as he gets a sufficiently strong motive and begins to exercise the undeveloped brain cells controlling the faculties, they immediately respond. Merely arousing a boy's ambition develops in him a great many deficient qualities by putting them into healthy exercise.

Change of environment will often wondrously develop a backward boy whose parents were completely discouraged with him under the home conditions. As soon as the boy got into a store, or into a school, or was thrown upon his own resources, his whole character was changed.

Various means which parents may employ in forming the characters of their children are formulated by Dr. A. T. Schofield, and may be summarized as follows: Forming habits of moral value; controlling environment so that suggestions of good—physical, mental, and moral—and not of evil are ever unconsciously sowing themselves in its brain; by example and story filling the child with inspiring ideals, so as to give direction to its will and energy of growth to its character; feeding the child's mind with proper ideas; exercising the growing moral powers with circumstances, so that overcoming and courage may be learned, and hardships endured, yet not too great to prove discouraging; balancing the various tendencies one against the other so as to prevent undue leaning in any one direction; strengthening the will to carry out its own designs and act with energy and decision; educating the moral sense and keeping it sensitive to evil; increasing the sense of responsibility to oneself, to others, and to God.

In attempting to apply such processes to oneself, what must be avoided is morbid introspection, or brooding over faults and means to get rid of them. Use then the method of cultivating the opposites, keeping the mind full of bright, hopeful, loving, uplifting thoughts, and expressing them all in deeds.

XVI. STRENGTHENING DEFICIENT FACULTIES

XVI. STRENGTHENING DEFICIENT FACULTIES

"What wouldst thou? All is thine—
The ways are opening for thee,
The light of truth doth shine;
Then halt not, question not;
Be still, and assert the I."

FEW people are well-balanced, well-rounded. A great many have splendid ability in certain lines, good education, fine training, and yet have some deficiency in their make-up which cripples the whole life and dwarfs the results of their utmost industry.

Many of us have some little, contemptible weakness which offsets our strong qualities and ruins their effectiveness.

How humiliating it is to be conscious that one has dragged up to maturity some such weakness or deficiency without realizing it, or at least without having it remedied. The deficiency is slight, perhaps, and yet, if it cripples life, if it mars achievement, if it is a perpetual humiliation, if it submits us to a thousand embarrassments and keeps us from rising in the world, what a terrible misfortune it is!

What a pity to see a giant in possibility tied down by some little, contemptible weakness which cripples what might have been a magnificent career! If parent or teacher would only point out to a child a weakness which, perhaps, will be fatal if not remedied, and teach it how to guard against it, how to strengthen the defective quality by mental exercise, what a tremendous help it would give to the child, perhaps preserving it from failure.

It is pitiable to see a young man bowing to what he calls fate, which he thinks has been fixed by the contour of his brain or in his hereditary tendencies. Why should we drag our weaknesses through life when a little common-sense, a little right thinking in fixing new habits of thought, would soon remedy them?

If you are conscious of a mental weakness, a deficient faculty, using a little concentration, thinking in the opposite direction, and dwelling upon the perfect faculties or qualities you desire would soon put you in a normal condition. It is normal thinking that makes the normal life.

But if you leave your weak faculties alone

DEFICIENT FACULTIES

—do not exercise them, do not try to enlarge them—how can you expect them ever to become strong? You cannot develop a symmetrical body by simply exercising the arms. The same is true of the mental faculties. Those which are not used deteriorate. If you long for a thing and strive for it with all your might persistently enough and long enough, you cannot help approximating it; you must get what you wish in some degree.

If your call for wisdom is loud enough and persistent enough, you will become wise. If you call for idleness and mere pleasure, you will get them; but you must not expect wisdom while you are struggling for another goal.

If you wish health, say health, think health, hold the picture of yourself in health before your mind as the sculptor holds that of the statue he is carving from the marble; hold it persistently and you will create health.

Do you wish relief from poverty? Hold the idea of plenty to use, to enjoy, not to hoard, not to oppress, but to bless, and it will as surely come to you as a rose from a bud.

"Affirm that which you wish, and it will manifest in your life."

If, for example, melancholia, taking too

serious a view of things, is your **fatal weakness**, you can entirely remedy this condition in a little while by perpetually concentrating the thought upon the bright, cheerful, sunny side of things. If you persist in this, after a while you will seldom have a depressing, gloomy thought. When you do, fling it out of your mind. Thrust it out as you would the thief from your house. Because a burglar gets into your room, is that any reason why you should let him stay there? Fling open the shutters and let in the light, and the gloom will disappear.

It is not difficult to do this; but every time you nurse the weakness or harbor the thought that depresses you, you make friends with it and invite it to stay. When you dwell upon the dark side of things, then you are encouraging everything which is darkening your life and hampering your career.

If you hold persistently in the mind the picture of the normal faculty which corresponds to the one you think is deficient, you will soon bring about the desired results.

I wish it were possible to show young people what a tremendous power for good there is in forming the habit of stoutly affirming **and** claiming desired qualities as one's birth-

DEFICIENT FACULTIES

right, with all the determination to possess them that can be mustered. The mere assumption of a thing with all our will power, and the determination to possess it which knows no retreat, are wonderful helps in achieving the things that we long for. Do not be afraid of claiming and repeating over and over again the qualities you long to attain or the object of your ambition. Keep your desire in the forefront of your thought. Resolve that you will possess these things and will accept nothing else, and you will be surprised to see how rapidly you will make yourself a magnet to draw the things you yearn for.

If you long for a beautiful character, claim it, assume it, stick to it with all possible tenacity, and you will not only prepare the mind to receive it, but will also increase the power of the mind to attract it.

We all know that in some way, somehow, most people get the things they long for and struggle for persistently. And even if they do not get all that they desire, they approximate much nearer to it, get much more of it than they would if they did not claim it stoutly and struggle for it persistently. We have the ability to change our attractive power, to increase it or diminish it, just in proportion to the intensity of our yearning for it and assuming it as our birthright.

Many people become morbid in dwelling upon the thought that they are peculiar in some respect. Some of these people think that they have inherited certain tendencies or peculiarities from their parents, and are always looking for their appearance in themselves. Now this is just the way to make them appear; for what we encourage in the mind or hold there persistently we get. So these people continually increase the evil by worrying about it and dwelling upon its sad effects on themselves. They become sensitive about their idiosyncrasies. They never like to speak of or hear of them, and yet the very consciousness that they possess them takes away their self-confidence and mars their achievement.

Now the great majority of these abnormalities and peculiarities are simply imaginary—or are exaggerated by imagination. They have been nursed and brooded over as possibilities so long that they become real to the sufferers. The remedy lies in doing precisely the opposite—dwelling on the perfect qualities, and ignoring any possible shortcomings.

If you think you are peculiar, form the habit of holding the normal thought. Say to yourself: " I am not peculiar. These seeming idiosyncrasies are not real. I was made in the image of my Maker, and a Perfect Being could not make imperfections; hence my imperfections cannot be real, as the truth of my being is real. There can be no abnormalities about me unless I produce them in thought, for the Creator never gave them to me. He never gave me a discordant note, because He is harmony."

If by holding this thought persistently in your mind you forget what seems abnormal to you, it will soon disappear, and you will regain your confidence just by becoming convinced that you are not much unlike other people.

Shyness sometimes becomes a disease; but it is a disease of the imagination only, and can be easily overcome by driving the thought of it out of the mind and holding the opposite thought; by just making up your mind that you are not being watched by everybody, that people are too busy about their own selfish aims and ambitions to be watching you.

XVII. GAIN BEAUTY BY HOLDING THE BEAUTY THOUGHT

XVII. GAIN BEAUTY BY HOLDING THE BEAUTY THOUGHT

Every right action and true thought sets the seal of its beauty on person and face.—RUSKIN.

IT is perfectly possible for a girl with the homeliest face, with the ugliest expression, if she has an honest heart, to make herself beautiful to every one who knows her by the perpetual habit of holding in her mind the beauty thought; not the thought of mere superficial beauty, but that of heart beauty, soul beauty. The basis of all real beauty is a kindly, helpful heart, and a desire to scatter sunshine and good cheer everywhere, and this, shining through the face, makes it beautiful. The longing and the effort to be beautiful in character cannot fail to make the life beautiful, and since the outward is but an expression of the inward, a mere outpicturing on the body of the habitual thought and dominating motives, the face, the manners, the bearing, must follow the thought, and become sweet and attractive. If you hold the beauty thought, the love thought, persist-

ently in the mind, you will make such an impression of harmony, of sweetness, and soul beauty wherever you go that no one will notice any plainness or deformity you may possess.

The highest beauty—beauty that is far superior to mere regularity of features—is within the reach of everybody. I know girls who have dwelt upon what they consider their unfortunate plainness so long that they have seriously exaggerated it. They are not half so plain as they think they are; and were it not for the fact that they have made themselves very sensitive and self-conscious about it, others would not notice it at all. In fact, if they could get rid of their sensitiveness and be natural, they could, with persistent effort, make up in sprightliness of thought, in cheerfulness of manner, in intelligence, and in cheery helpfulness what they lack in grace and beauty of face.

I have known a girl whose extreme plainness of features and awkwardness of manner so pained her as she approached womanhood that she almost despaired of ever making anything of herself, and even contemplated suicide. She was so convinced that she was a target for cruel remarks, and became so impressed with the conviction that she was not wanted anywhere, and that she was continually being insulted, that she resolved to make one supreme effort to redeem herself from her handicap. She resolved that she would make people love her, that she would attract them instead of repelling them; that she would take such an unselfish interest in them that they could not help loving her. She determined to develop those beautiful heart qualities which would more than compensate for mere physical beauty. She began to sympathize with people and to take thought of their welfare. Wherever she went, if she saw any one who was ill at ease or looked troubled or friendless, she immediately took such a deep interest in him that she won his friendship at once. She began to cultivate her mind in every possible way in order to make herself interesting, bright, cheerful, and hopeful. She cultivated optimism, and she was soon surprised to see how the young people who formerly shunned her flocked around her, and began to love her; and she not only succeeded in compensating for her physical deformity, which she thought was fatal to her pleasure and her usefulness, but she also developed a soul beauty that did not pass with years, and which was infinitely superior to that beauty which comes from regularity of features and beauty of form. She seemed to radiate good cheer from every pore. So popular did she become that the so-called pretty girls envied her.

XVIII. THE POWER OF IMAGINATION

XVIII. THE POWER OF IMAGINATION

"Imagination precedes and is the cause of all achievement."

E owe the improvement of the world, the climb to civilization, largely to the imagination. We should still be living as savages in caves and huts but for those who could imagine and were determined to have better things.

Indeed, the men and women who have rendered the greatest service to the world have done so by seeing in their imaginations something infinitely better than actually existed, and then working to make this real.

It was because Morse saw in his imagination a better way of communication than by post that he was enabled to give the telegraph to the world. It was because Bell could imagine something better even than the telegraph that we have the telephone. It was because Field could see in his imagination a better way of communicating across the ocean than by ship that continents are tied together with cables. It was because Marconi saw even a better way of communicating than anything that had gone before that we have the wireless telegraph which enables a passenger when in mid-ocean to engage his hotel room and order a cab to meet the steamer.

An unknown Greek sculptor gave us in the Venus of Milo a suggestion of possible beauty of proportion and magnificence of pose up to which the race has not yet measured. But it gave us a model toward which we are still struggling, and toward which the race has made a great advance.

What does the world not owe to the magnificent imagination of Michael Angelo, who, in that wonderful statue of Moses, gave a glimpse of the possible godlike man.

It was the imagination of great composers that gave us our masterpieces in music.

It was because merchants imagined a hundred kinds of business under one roof that we have great department stores where people can buy almost anything they need.

It is because teachers could see in imagination a chance for infinite improvement in the human race that we have our schools and our colleges. Indeed, what do we not owe to the imagination? The men who see things only as they are, who have no imaginations, plod along in the same old ruts. It is the man with imagination that improves things, that advances, that substitutes the palace cars for the stage-coach, the ocean greyhound for the sailing ship.

It is because our great artists saw something better in imagination than actually existed in nature that we have some of our greatest masterpieces. It is not enough to see nature as she is; it is infinitely higher to see her, in the imagination, as she is capable of becoming; to see her possibilities as realities.

The average person thinks the imaginative person amounts to nothing. He is called a **crank**. Dreamers are looked upon as impractical people, mere theorists; but oftentimes our dreamers have proved infinitely more practical than those who have laughed at them, for the world's dreamers have given us the most practical things we have. The dreamers have ameliorated the hard conditions of the race, have lifted us above commonness and emancipated us from drudgery.

Oh, what does the world not owe **to** its dreamers, to its cranks, to its theorists?

Great characters have been made possible because men and women saw greater men and women in themselves than actually existed.

It was their struggle to bring out the possible man or the possible woman that advanced civilization. It is because fathers and mothers can see in their imagination human beings higher than themselves, more perfect, and more complete, that they are able to lift their children above themselves.

The time will come when we shall realize what a tremendous subjective power the imagination has upon life; what a tremendous factor it can be made in education, in forming ideals, in influencing the career, and in promoting health and happiness.

The pictures of the mind are not given to mock us or to entertain us, but to show us that they can be made realities, that there is a reality that imagines them; that these are but the outlines or the suggestions, the shadows of the realities themselves.

They make us real seers of the possible future, and are given us to whet our ambition, to spur us on, to make us dissatisfied with the commonness in which we are living by giving us glimpses of something infinitely better.

We are beginning to see that imagination is not mere fantasy of the brain, but that in it lives the ideal, in it are generated the great models and the potencies which make their realization possible.

If the imagination of a child can be rightly directed, its future happiness and success can be assured; but a perverted imagination may bring misery and gloom untold.

The training of the imagination of a child so as to form the habit of producing beautiful pictures instead of hideous ones, perpetually inspiring images instead of demoralizing ones, and thus harmony instead of discord, would be of more value to him than to give him a fortune.

XIX. DON'T LET THE YEARS COUNT

XIX. DON'T LET THE YEARS COUNT

"The face cannot betray the years until the mind has given its consent. The mind is the sculptor."

 SAY to the years as I have said to the public, '*Quand même*, I shall conquer you.'" There speaks a spirit that will never grow old; and who that has recently seen Sarah Bernhardt can doubt that, as time passes, she continues to make good her challenge to the years, "*Quand même*." At threescore, the great actress is in the prime of her powers, and does not look a day over forty.

It is not by any particular grace of nature that Madame Bernhardt and many others who are more advanced in years than she retain their youth, but because of their attitude toward the years. They refuse to let them count. They have made up their minds that they will not grow old in the ordinary sense.

"Better than the art of growing old gracefully is the secret of not growing old at all," says a writer in the Chicago *Journal*. "It is something worth knowing and worth remembering. The secret is concealed in the fact that men and women are as old as they make themselves to be. That implies will power, but what of it? The world is governed by will power."

Julia Ward Howe is a splendid example of youthful activity and mental vigor and freshness in old age. So was Mary A. Livermore until her recent death. Henry Gassoway Davis, recently the octogenarian nominee of the Democratic party for the vice-presidency, exhibits an elasticity and vigor of mind and body that put many a man of forty to shame. George Meredith, on the celebration of his seventy-fourth birthday, said: "I do not feel that I am growing old either in heart or mind. I still look on life with a young man's eye. I have always hoped that I would not grow old as some, with a palsied intellect, living backward, regarding other people as anachronisms, because they themselves have lived on in the other time and left their sympathies behind them with their years."

When a man becomes wise enough to recognize his own divinity—that he is as indestructible a principle as a law of mathematics; that no accident of life, no friction, trouble, or difficulty can touch the divine part of him; and when he recognizes the truth of being, that he is a part of the infinite creative principle, he will not begin to show signs of mental and physical decrepitude when he should be in the prime of all his powers.

Age will never succeed in retaining a youthful appearance and mentality until people make up their minds not to let the years count; until they cease to make the body old by constant suggestions of the mind. We begin to sow seed thoughts of age in youth. We look forward to being old at forty-five, and to going down hill at fifty.

The very act of preparing for old age hastens it. As Job said, "The thing I feared most has come upon me." People who prepare for a thing and look for it, anticipating, fearing, dreading it in their daily lives, usually get it.

"Any person continually in fear of something will bear the marks of such fear graven in his or her face," says Prentice Mulford. "If you so look forward to such decay of the body as a thing that must come, it will come."

Never for a moment allow yourself to think that you are too old to do this or that, for your thoughts and convictions will very soon outpicture themselves in a wrinkled face and a prematurely old expression. There is nothing better established than the philosophy that we are what we think, and that we become like our thoughts.

"How old are you?" asks the Milwaukee *Journal.* "The adage is that women are as old as they look and men as old as they feel. That's wrong. A man and a woman are as old as they make themselves to be. Growing old is largely a habit of the mind. 'As a man thinketh in his heart so is he.' If he begins shortly after middle age to imagine himself growing old, he will be old. To keep oneself from decrepitude is somewhat a matter of will power. The fates are kind to the man who hangs onto life with both hands. He who lets go will go. Death is slow to tackle only the tenacious. Ponce de Leon searched in the wrong place for the fountain of youth. It is in oneself. One must keep oneself young inside, so that while 'the outer man perisheth the inner man is renewed day by day.' When the human mind ceases to exert itself, when there is no longer an active interest in the affairs of this life, when the human stops reading and thinking and doing, the man, like a blasted tree, begins to die at the top. You are as old as you think you are. **Keep the harness on. Your job is not done.**"

> "'Tis yet high day, thy staff resume,
>   And fight fresh battle for the truth;
> For what is age but youth's full bloom,
>   A riper, more transcendent youth,"

sings Oliver Wendell Holmes.

If you would live long, love your work and continue doing it. Don't lay it down at fifty because you think your powers are on the wane, or that you need a rest. Take a vacation whenever you require it, but don't give up your work. There is life, there is youth in it. "I cannot grow old," says a noted actress, "because I love my art. I spend my life absorbed in it. I am never bored. How can one have lines of age or weariness or discontent when one is happy, busy, never fatigued, and one's spirit is ever, ever young? When I am tired it is not my soul, but just my body." Think of Susan B. Anthony, the veteran reformer, in her eighty-third year, and of Mrs. Gilbert, the veteran actress, who died on reaching the same age! Who thinks of these splendid workers as old, or failing, or left behind by younger competitors? Miss Anthony is as vigorous and full of enthusiasm in her work to-day as she was half a century ago. At the International Congress of Women, held in Berlin, she was easily the most prominent among the representative women of the world gathered there, and one of the most active. Mrs. Gilbert, long the oldest actress on the stage, in her last season " starred " in a new play. These women never thought of laying down their work or of growing old at fifty or sixty. They found the great drama of humanity too interesting to give up their parts.

" One of the finest things about our generation," says Margaret Deland, " is an awakening to the fact that age ought to be only a matter of the body, a matter of spectacles and stiff joints, not of dulness and distaste for living, not of days in which we shall say we have no pleasure in them. There is a growing belief that this second age can be avoided: nay, more, with some high natures there is even a realization that such age is a confession of sin, a confession that life has been selfish, narrow, unimaginative, and without living ideals. Such age is shame. Little by little this belief is growing in human creatures."

The sentiment is expressed in these verses by Frank M. Vancil:

DON'T LET YEARS COUNT

"Never grow old. Time's furrowed lines
  Of pain, of sorrow, and of tears
Must leave their impress, wide and deep,
  On the face of declining years.

"But the gentle spirit, fraught with love—
  Bright deeds of happiness unfold;
Grows brighter, lovelier with age—
  More winsome still—grows never old."

"We do not count a man's years," said Emerson, "until he has nothing else to count." It is not the years that age us so much as the use we make of them, and the way we live them. Excesses of any kind are fatal to longevity or the prolongation of youth.

Bitter memories of a sinful life which has gone all wrong make premature furrows in the face, take the brightness from the eyes and the elasticity from the step, and make one's life sapless and uninteresting.

The Bible teaches that a clean life, a pure life, a simple life, and a useful life shall be long. "His flesh shall be fresher than a child's. He shall return to the days of his youth."

It is the useless complexities in which vanity and unworthy ambition entangle us that wear away life and make so many Americans old men and women at forty. The simple life can be the fullest, noblest, and most useful. Rev. Charles Wagner says that a simple life and a strenuous life are not inconsistent, as a peaceful life and a vigorous life are not. In his little book, "The Simple Life," he shows most effectively how our needless complexities of thought and feeling cause us to waste energies that should be concentrated on useful ends. He emphasizes the fact that by our worrying and vexation of spirit we rob ourselves of vigor that, rightly employed, would accomplish valuable results.

"In this age of rush, hurry, and tumbling over each other, thousands imagine it is necessary to be doing something all one's waking (or we will say business) hours to attain success. Leisure is almost a sin. This is a great mistake," says Prentice Mulford. "Thousands on thousands are so 'doing' all the time. What does their 'doing' amount to? A pittance, a bare subsistence, and why? Because there is no discretion as to what the person's force is put upon. One woman wears her body out at forty in polishing stoves, scrubbing tinware, and in hundreds of other little jobs. Her mind is all absorbed in these details. Another

DON'T LET YEARS COUNT

one sits quietly and an idea comes to her whereby all this work may be accomplished without any physical effort on her part, and by those who can do nothing else. She is the more likely to preserve her health and vigor. Health and vigor are the belongings of a relatively perfect maturity that is even more attractive than what is generally called youth.

"It is a great aid to the preservation of youth and vigor to be able to sit still and keep still in mind as well as in body when there is really nothing to do, because in such condition mind and body are recuperating and filling up with new force. The body is not fed with material food alone. There are other elements, now little recognized, which act upon it and give it strength, and the grand source and means of receiving these lie partly in that mental and physical quietude of mind which acts only when it has full power to act. If, then, wisdom guides action either by brain or hand, a great deal more is accomplished and a balance of life's forces is kept in reserve."

Few people realize, also, that the day processes, unless checked, still go on while we sleep. If you have been running worry thoughts, fretting thoughts, anxious thoughts, pessimistic thoughts, hard, jealous, envious, greedy thoughts through your mind during the day, you may be sure that these will run their deadly course in the brain far into the night, furrowing their tracks deeper and deeper in the nervous tissue, exhausting nerve force and vitality, and that they will outpicture themselves in the face by deepening the lines, by making more prominent and permanent the wrinkles. Many people are so constituted that the moment they are free from absorbing duties their troubles and trials flock into their minds and fill their imaginations with hideous pictures, robbing them of all joy, and spontaneity, and happiness.

The moment they lie down at night their minds begin to work to their injury. Their imaginations magnify the dark pictures, the disagreeable experiences, and they toss upon their beds until they go to sleep from sheer exhaustion in this unhappy frame of mind. Is it any wonder that they age rapidly; that they get up in the morning tired and exhausted; that they have to resort to all sorts of artificial sedatives to make them sleep; that they are always taking tonics or stimulants to keep themselves in condition to work?

We shall some time learn that the mind is its own tonic when we know how to use it;

that it is its own best stimulant; that when we live normally we shall not need narcotics or drugs of any kind; that the mind will be its own best protector, its own rejuvenator. It is only a question of holding the mind right, of holding the harmonious thought, the cheerful thought, the helpful thought, the love thought, and while these dominate the mind, the enemy thoughts which tear down and destroy cannot enter. We should be able to shut off all the day processes which grind out the life, and which exhaust the nerve force and the brain energy, and the moment we quit our business we should begin to build up, to recuperate for the next day; to fill up the cask again for the next demand.

I know a few people who have learned the supreme art of preparing for a sweet, peaceful, restful, refreshing sleep by reversing the brain processes which have perplexed them and bothered them during the day. They have learned the secret of shutting out all their troubles, trials, and perplexities, of locking them in the store, or office, or factory when they turn the key at night. They never drag their business troubles home. They consider themselves at play from the moment they leave work until they get back again. Nothing can induce them to be bothered or bored with anything relating to business. They have learned the secret and power of the harmonious thought, the happy thought, the cheerful, optimistic thought. They prepare their minds for a serene, harmonious night's sleep by summoning thoughts of joy, youth, peace, and love to be their mind guests for the night, and will entertain no others. They will not allow the old worry thought and anxious thought to drag their hideous images through the brain to spoil their rest and to leave ugly autographs in the face. The result is that they get up in the morning refreshed, rejuvenated, with all the spontaneity of their youth.

We grow old because we do not know enough to keep young, just as we become sick and diseased because we do not know enough to keep well. Sickness is a result of ignorance and wrong thinking. The time will come when a man will no more harbor thoughts that will make him sick or weak than he would think of putting his hands into the fire. No man can be ill if he always has right thoughts and takes ordinary care of his body. If he will think only useful thoughts he can maintain his youth far beyond the usual period.

Never smother the impulse to act in a youthful manner because you think you are too old. Recently, at a family gathering, the boys were trying to get their father, past sixty, to play with them. "Oh, go away, go away!" he said; "I am too old for that." But the mother entered into their sports, apparently with just as much enthusiasm and real delight as if she were only their age. The youthful spirit shone in her eyes and manifested itself in every movement. Her frolic with the boys explains why she looks so much younger than her husband, in spite of the very slight difference in their years.

Be always as young as you feel, and keep young by associating with young people, and taking an interest in their interests, hopes, plans, and amusements. The vitality of youth is contagious.

When questioned as to the secret of his marvellous youthfulness, in his eightieth year, Oliver Wendell Holmes replied that it was due chiefly "to a cheerful disposition and invariable contentment in every period of my life with what I was. I never felt the pangs of ambition, discontent, and disquietude that make us grow old prematurely by carving wrinkles in our faces. Wrinkles do not appear on faces that have constantly smiled. Smiling is the best possible massage. Contentment is the fountain of youth."

We need to practise the contentment extolled by the genial doctor, which is not the contentment of inertness, but the freeing of ourselves from entangling vanities, petty cares, worries, and anxieties, which hamper us in our real life-work. The sort of ambition he condemns is that in which egotism and vanity figure most conspicuously, and in which notoriety, the praise and admiration of the world, wealth, and personal aggrandizement are the objects sought, rather than the power to be of use in the world, to be a leader in the service of humanity, and to be the noblest, best, and most efficient worker that one can be.

If you would " be young when old," adopt the sundial's motto—" I record none but the hours of sunshine." Never mind the dark or shadowed hours. Forget the unpleasant, unhappy days. Remember only the days of rich experiences; let the others drop into oblivion.

It is said that " long livers are great hopers." If you keep your hope bright in spite of discouragements, and meet all difficulties with a cheerful face, it will be very difficult for age to trace its furrows on your brow. There is longevity in cheerfulness.

"Don't let go of love, or love of romance; they are amulets against wrinkles." If the mind is constantly bathed in love, and filled with helpful, charitable sentiments toward all, the body will keep fresh and vigorous many years longer than it will if the heart is dried up and emptied of human sympathy by a greedy life. The heart that is kept warm by love is never frozen by age or chilled by prejudice, fear, or anxious thought. A French beauty used to have herself massaged with mutton tallow every night in order to keep her muscles elastic and her body supple. A better way of preserving youthful elasticity is coming into vogue, massaging the mind with love thoughts, beauty thoughts, cheerful thoughts, and young ideals.

If you do not want the years to count, look forward instead of backward, and put as much variety and as many interests into your life as possible. Monotony and lack of mental occupation are great age producers. Women who live in cities in the midst of many interests and great variety, preserve their youth and good looks, as a rule, much longer than women who live in remote country places, who get no variety into their lives, and who have no interests outside of their narrow, daily round of monotonous duties, which require no exercise of mind. Insanity is an alarmingly increasing result of monotony of women's lives on the farm. Ellen Terry and Sarah Bernhardt, "who seem to have the ageless brightness of the stars," attribute their youthfulness to action, change of thought and scene, and mental occupation. It is worth noting, too, that farmers who live so much outdoors, and in an environment much more healthful than that of the average brain-worker, do not live so long as the latter.

Indeed, a physician testifying in the London law courts stated that softening of the brain was a common malady of the rural laborers of England. Their brains, he said, rather rusted out from lack of brain exercise, than wore out, and at an age from sixty-five to seventy-five they usually died of apoplexy or some similar disease. In contrast to the farmers, he cited judges and similar hard brain-workers who lived much longer and kept their mental powers.

When Solon, the Athenian sage, was asked the secret of his strength and youth, he replied that it was "learning something new every day." This belief was general among the ancient Greeks—that the secret of eternal youth is "to be always learning something new."

There is the basis of a great truth in the idea. It is healthful activity that strengthens and preserves the mind as well as the body, and gives it youthful quickness and activity. So if you would be young, in spite of the years, you must remain receptive to new thought and must grow broader in spirit, wider in sympathy, and more and more open to fresh revelations of truth as you travel farther on the road of life.

But the greatest conqueror of age is a cheerful, hopeful, loving spirit. A man who would conquer the years must have charity for all. He must avoid worry, envy, malice, and jealousy; all the small meannesses that feed bitterness in the heart, trace wrinkles on the brow, and dim the eye. A pure heart, a sound body, and a broad, healthy, generous mind, backed by a determination not to let the years count, constitute a fountain of youth which every one may find in himself.

"Here, then," says Margaret Deland, "are the three deadly symptoms of old age: selfishness, stagnation, intolerance. If we find them in ourselves, we may know we are growing old—even if we are on the merry side of thirty. But, happily, we have three defences, which are invulnerable; if we use them, we shall die young if we live to be a hundred. They are: sympathy, progress, tolerance. The men or women who have these divine qualities of sympathy, progress, and tolerance are forever young; their very existence cries out to the rest of us, *sursum corda!*"

> "*The best is yet to be!*
> *The last of life*
> *For which the first was made.*"

XX. HOW TO CONTROL THOUGHT

XX. HOW TO CONTROL THOUGHT

Ordain for thyself forthwith a certain form and type of conduct, which thou shalt maintain, both alone, and, when it may chance, among men.—EPICTETUS.

IT is possible to change the character of the mind by habitually controlling the thought. There is no reason why we should allow the mind to wander into all sorts of fields, and to dwell upon all sorts of subjects at random. The ego, the will power, or what we call the real self, the governor of the mind, can dominate the thought. With a little practice, we can control and concentrate the mind in any reasonable way we please.

Attention, therefore, controlled by the will and directed by reason and higher judgment, can so discipline the mind and thought that they will dwell on higher ideals, until high thinking has become a habit. Then the lower ideals and lower thinking will drop out of consciousness, and the mind will be left upon a higher plane. It is only a question of discipline.

Many and varied are the methods prescribed by various writers for gaining desired thought control, but on comparing them there is, after all, much in common, and that is the simplest and most practical part. The more elaborate formulæ and mysticism may be left to those who enjoy such exercises.

"It is not possible to give explicit directions for an American substitute for Hindu Yoga practice," says W. J. Colville, "as the general needs of the Anglo-Saxon race are not the same outwardly as those of their dark-skinned Oriental brethren; but the great words *concentration* and *meditation* are just as forceful and full of meaning in the West as in the East. To concentrate on one's beloved goal, to see before the mental eye the prize as though it were already won, while we are all the while intensely conscious of moving nearer to its externalization, is so to place ourselves in relation with all that helps us on our way, that one by one obstacles vanish, and what seemed once too hard for human strength to accomplish appears now plain and even simple. The greatest need of all is to keep the goal in sight and not let interest flag or inward vision waver.

"A good lesson for all to practise is to take some special aspiration into the silence, and there realize its fulfillment with all the intensity of your visualistic ability. See yourself in the very place in which you most desire to be engaged, in the very work you would love best to accomplish. A little persistent industry in this exercise will soon relieve the intellect of worry, and gradually open up the understanding to perceive how to accomplish the otherwise unaccomplishable. There is no substitute for work in all the universe, therefore let none imagine that a state of inoperative, dreamy contemplation is one to be recommended. Outward work must follow inward contemplation. True meditation does not absolve us from the need of making effort, but it is a means for revealing to us what efforts we need to make and how to make them."

Something the same process is recommended by a writer who says: " Go into the silence, concentrate your mind, polarize thought, breathe in the power and strength that is ever within the reach of all, and in unlimited supply, from which nothing but our own action or rejection can cut us off."

" The atmosphere about us is a product of thought. Thought makes it what it is, and thought alone can change it when it will," says Floyd B. Wilson, in " Paths to Power." " The atmosphere that marks strong individuality is universally conceded to be the product of the invisible emanation of thought centred on an idea. Your atmosphere, being a product of thought, must receive all its power and force through the creative energy that gives it existence.

"Our proposition as to control, therefore, now reduces itself to this: If we know ourselves masters of our mental apparatus, we know we can control our thoughts and thus dictate our atmosphere. If, in silence, daily, we hold ourselves passive—receptive for the particular good we most desire—we open the way for the creation of the atmosphere that is sought. One must come to these sittings as nearly passive as possible; but above all free from doubt. To many it will be found serious work to learn to hold themselves passive. The moments spent in this way will do more to advance you to the end than any other thing you can do."

Speaking more especially of the means of controlling the thought for the benefit of the body, Charles Brodie Patterson says: "Let us keep the mind clear and bright, fill it with wholesome thoughts of life, and be kindly in our feelings toward others. Let us have no fear of anything, but realize that we are one with universal power—that power which can supply our every need; that health, strength, and happiness are our legitimate birthright, that they are ever potential in our inner lives, and that our bodies may express them now. If we take this mental attitude and adhere steadfastly to it, the body will very soon manifest health and strength."

In the light of these various directions from those who have drawn them from the experience of themselves and of others, it does not seem so difficult for one to raise his standard of living very materially by forcing into his thoughts the higher and forcing out the lower.

If you surround yourself with a positive atmosphere, that is, if you keep all negatives, all destroyers, all thoughts that suggest discord, disease, disaster, and failure out of your mind, and hold there only those words and thoughts which create, which upbuild, you will very soon change the character of your entire mind, so that you will loathe the enemies of your success and happiness, and will **thrust them out of your mind the moment they attempt to enter; you will harbor only noble words and thoughts, those which en-**

courage, which bring light and beauty, which inspire and ennoble, and you will welcome these as eagerly as you shun the others.

It is encouraging, too, that thinkers and investigators have traced the origin of our thought enemies back to their sources and have thus reduced their number.

"It is not necessary to engage in battle the small army of lesser passions," says Horace Fletcher, "if you concentrate your efforts against anger and worry, for they are all children of these parents. Oppose them with a bold front; make one heroic stand against them, and they and all their children will fly. Disown them once and the ability to readopt them will have disappeared with them." In a later book, Mr. Fletcher calls anger and worry only forms of fear, and W. W. Atkinson also says: "Worry is the child of Fear, and bears a strong family resemblance to its parent. Treat the Fear family as you would any other kind of vermin—get rid of the old ones before they have a chance to have progeny." So once we gain the power of concentration we must cultivate perfect fearlessness and confidence, with which go cheerfulness, efficiency, and, as a sure result, happiness and prosperity.

The following rules in "Power of Will," by Frank C. Haddock, are practical and suggestive, and may well close this chapter:

"Resolutely, persistently, and intelligently maintain a true and psychic field by constant exercise of strong will power toward all high realities: beautiful objects, right ideas, health, peace, truth, success, altruism, right-minded persons, the best literature, art, science, the noblest movements and institutions of the times, and a true religion.

"In contact with other people, maintain in your personal atmosphere a perfect and constant calm. Let this be so complete that it may not betray the effort to secure it, either in disturbed ether waves, or in movements which the other person's subconsciousness will recognize as coolness or suppressed hostility.

"Avoid all excitement.

"Send out no antagonisms.

"Reveal to the inner consciousness of other people nothing in your mind calculated to injure their feelings.

"Banish from your field all feelings of contempt and ridicule.

"Permit no vibrations of anger or irritation to escape into your field.

"Banish absolutely all thought waves of fear for persons with whom you are dealing.

"Banish all thought waves of distrust as to success with such persons.

"Maintain a personal atmosphere that is surcharged with the dynamic force of confident expectancy."

XXI. THE COMING MAN WILL REALIZE HIS DIVINITY

XXI. THE COMING MAN WILL REALIZE HIS DIVINITY

All the mysteries are cleared away and solved as we come into oneness with the Blessed One and begin to know—begin to be omniscient. Many omniscient men will soon walk the earth. Omniscience and freedom are the goal of *all*, and in this Great Age of Light many Egos are approaching the blessed omniscient state. He who sees God in *All* feels the ecstatic and blissful thrill of the Infinite Presence that cannot be described. How beautiful is the Universe to him who is at one with God and knows the Planner and the Plan.—THE BLISSFUL PROPHET.

A HAPPY, contented, successful career must flow from a well-balanced, symmetrical mind, which has a sense of absolute security and unquestioned faith in the Great Creator, the providing and sustaining power.

A sense of uncertainty, of uneasiness, a lack of poise, of equilibrium in the life, is fatal to high success. We must think deeply enough into the nature of things to get rid of uncertainties. We must be rooted in the truth of being, and feel an unwavering faith that we are a part of the great Mind which creates and governs all things. There is a sense of certainty, of absolute security, when we know that nothing can wrench us out of our orbit, that no accident on land or sea, no disease or discord, can separate us from our union with that great power. Once having this security, fear departs, uncertainty and anxiety leave us, and all the faculties work in harmony. When we know that nothing can cheat us out of our birthright, that nothing can mar our real achievement, that every right step must lead to ultimate triumph, that every right act, that every germ of goodness, will ultimately struggle into flower and fruitage, we can serenely accomplish the highest that lies in our power.

There is something in our very consciousness which tells us that we are not mere products of chance. We feel that there is a certainty somewhere; that fear, anxiety, and uncertainty are not a necessary part of life. There is an instinct within us which tells us that we are inseparable from the one great Mind, that we are one with it, a reflection of it, that we were created in its image, and that our ultimate purpose cannot conflict with its ultimate purpose. We instinctively feel that there must be a unity in all things, could we but find it, and the best way to find it is to trust this great power. Implicit faith will do more for us than reasoning, and will bring us infinitely closer to this unity.

These verses by Ella Wheeler Wilcox urge such exercise of faith:

"*Trust in thine own untried capacity*
  As thou wouldst trust in God himself. Thy
    soul
Is but an emanation from the whole.

"*Thou dost not dream what forces lie in thee,*
  Vast and unfathomed as the grandest sea.
  Thy silent mind o'er diamond caves may roll;
  Go seek them, but let Pilot Will control
  Those passions which thy favoring winds can be.

"*No man shall place a limit to thy strength;*
  Such triumphs as no mortal ever gained
  May yet be thine if thou wilt but believe
  In thy Creator and in thyself. At length
  Some feet will tread all heights now unattained—
  Why not thine own? Press on! achieve! achieve!"

When we once touch power, when we once feel the thrill of the great central force which comes from the heart of truth, of being, we shall no longer doubt, no longer hesitate, **no** longer be satisfied with the superficial, **the** temporary, the material. When the soul once tastes its native food, once feels the thrill of the infinite pulse, it no longer is content to grovel.

When a man realizes that he is divine, when he sees that he is a part of the everlasting principle which is the very essence of reality, nothing can throw him off his physical or mental balance. He is centred in the everlasting truth, intrenched there in infinite power from the taint of fear, or anxiety, or worry, or accident, because he is conscious that he is principle himself, a part of the eternal verity. The feeling that he is in touch with the power which made and upholds the universe, that nothing can wrench him from this divine presence, gives a sense of security and peace. When he awakens in the morning, refreshed and rejuvenated, he feels that he has been in touch with the divinity that created him; that he has passed the borderland of sense and has come into the presence of an infinite power, an infinite life; that he has been created anew, and hence when he is tired and weary and sad, how he longs to get back to this divine presence, to be made over, to quench his thirst at the great fountain-head of life.

Man will never attain his highest power until he learns that his principle is as indestructible, as impossible of harm, as the laws of mathematics. Suppose all the mathematical books in the world were destroyed by fire, two and two would still make four. The principle itself would not be in the least affected. So when the real man arrives at his dominion, he will not in the least be disturbed by anything that may happen; he will maintain his equanimity, his mental poise, through all sorts of disaster without a tremor. The Creator has not made a mistake; his highest creation is not placed at the mercy of chance or accident.

Serenity of spirit, poise of mind, is one of the last lessons of culture, and comes from a perfect trust in the all-controlling force of the universe. The moment man realizes that he is a part of a great cause, that he is made to dominate and not to be dominated, he will rise to meet every situation in a masterly instead of in a cringing manner.

When he comes to the full realization of his divinity, he will not be thrown from his base, nor will his peace be disturbed in the least by the vexatious happenings which trouble those who have not risen to their dominion, or who have not yet learned the secret of power.

"It is the greatest manifestation of power to be calm," says Swami Vivekanandi. "It is easy to be active. Let the reins go, and the horses will drag you down. Any one can do that; but he who can stop the plunging horses is the strong man. Which requires the greater strength—letting go, or restraining? The calm man is not the man who is dull. You must not mistake calmness for dulness or laziness. . . . Activity is the manifestation of the lower strength, calmness of the superior strength."

What have panics, or fires, or financial losses to do with the well-balanced man whom God made?

Suppose I should lose my property, what if my ships, my stores, and my houses should burn up, what has that really to do with me? It is true it may inconvenience me somewhat, and it may take some temporary power from my hand, but I cannot believe that an all-wise Creator has put my real self at the mercy of a panic, a fire, or any such emergency. Some people can so thoroughly impregnate themselves with thoughts of health, harmony, joy, gladness, and peace that accidents, misfortunes, and discordant moods cannot touch them.

I do not believe that the coming man, the ideal man, the man of the highest civilization, would be any more affected by a fire which destroyed his property than the laws of harmony would be affected by the burning up of all the musical instruments in the world.

The coming man will be so much master of his thought that he will be able to make himself one great magnet for attracting only those things which will add to his prosperity and enhance his happiness. He will be able to keep his body in perfect harmony by harboring only the health thought, and knowing how to exclude the disease thought, the sickly thought.

The coming man will always be cheerful, because he will entertain only the thoughts which produce happiness; he will not allow the clouds of worry or anxiety, or the darkness of melancholy, the blackness of jealousy and envy, to enter his mind. He will never mourn, but will always rejoice.

The coming man will no more allow the poisonous thoughts of pessimism, of disease, of wretchedness, of discord, to enter his mind, than he would take poisonous drugs into his stomach. He will be as able to control the kind and quality of his thoughts, as he is able to control the character of the guests he entertains in his home. He will invite only those he wants, only those whose influence he craves, and will exclude the enemy thoughts.

The coming man will not have the word "can't" in his vocabulary, for he will not have any doubt in his mind. The coming man will not know fear, which is now the greatest enemy of the human race, for he will not harbor the fear thought, which really results from a feeling of inefficiency, or inability to cope with the exigencies which may arise.

The coming man will always be prosperous because he will not allow the poverty thought, the limitation thought, to enter his mind. He will always hold thoughts of prosperity and abundance.

The coming man will live in an atmosphere of love and joyousness, for he himself will always feel and express love and joy. He will be healthy because soul and mind and body will be in that harmony which is perfect health.

Is it worth nothing to be able to think oneself out of discord into harmony, out of darkness into light, out of hatred into love, out of disease into health? Is it worth nothing to be able to rise into one's dominion, to reign as a sovereign instead of grovelling as an abject slave? Such an attainment is worthy of the highest aspiration and the greatest effort. What it may mean to an individual is beautifully expressed by Ralph Waldo Trine:

"With this awakening and realization one is brought at once *en rapport* with the universe. He feels the power and the thrill of life universal. He goes out from his own little garden spot, and mingles with the great universe; and the little perplexities, trials, and difficulties of life that to-day so vex and annoy him, fall away of their own accord by reason of their very insignificance. The intuitions become keener and ever more keen and unerring in their guidance. There comes more and more the power of reading men, so that no harm can come from this source. There comes more and more the power of seeing into the future, so that more and more true becomes the old adage that coming events cast their shadows before. Health in time takes the place of disease; for all disease and its consequent suffering is merely the result of the violation of law, whether consciously or unconsciously. There comes a spiritual power which, as it is sent out, is adequate for the healing of others the same as in the days of old. The body becomes less gross and heavy, finer in its texture and form, so that it serves far better and responds more readily to the higher impulses of the soul. Matter itself in time responds to the action of these higher forces; and many things that we are accustomed by reason of our limited vision to call miraculous or supernatural become the normal, the natural, the every-day."

The man who keeps his thoughts and his life tending upward will, in every emergency, find the forces of nature and of his fellow-men rushing to aid him, according to the law, "To him that hath, shall be given," and, because like produces like, the more one has of the success thought, the happiness thought, the good-will thought, the more powerful will be the attraction for kindred things. Thus all good things "shall be added unto him" and he shall become "perfect, even as your Father which is in heaven is perfect."

Opinions of
The Miracle of Right Thought

Dr. Sheldon Leavitt says:

"I wish to state that I am unusually well pleased with Dr. Marden's 'Miracle of Right Thought.' It is the best work of the author."

Ralph Waldo Trine says:

"This is one of those inspiring, reasonable and valuable books that are bringing new life and new power to so many thousands all over our country and all over the world to-day."

"You have formulated a philosophy

which must sooner or later be universally accepted. Your book shows how the right mental attitude helps one in the realization of every laudable ambition, and the value of cultivating a bright, self-reliant habit of thought. I congratulate you on it."
G. H. SANDISON, *Editor, The Christian Herald.*

"It is marked by sanctified common sense

it is in line with the advance thought of to-day, and yet it is so simple in statement that unlettered men and untrained youths can master its best thoughts and translate them into their daily lives."
REV. R. S. MACARTHUR, D.D., *New York City.*

Rev. F. E. Clark, President United Society of Christian Endeavor, says:

"I regard 'The Miracle of Right Thought' as one of Dr. Marden's very best books, and that is saying a great deal He has struck the modern note of the power of mind over bodily conditions in a fresh and most interesting way, while he has not fallen into the mistake of some New Thought writers of eliminating the personal God from the universe. No one can read this book sympathetically, I believe, without being happier and better."

```
12mo, cloth,           $1.00 net.   By mail, $1.10
Pocket Ed., silk,       1 25 net.   By mail,  1.33
Pocket Ed., leather,    1.50 net.   By mail,  1.58
```

THOMAS Y. CROWELL & CO., NEW YORK

Letters to Dr. Marden concerning

Getting On

Effective and Inspiring

"I think the chapters in this book are the most effective and inspiring I have read. They make one want to be something better. Had I read them ten or fifteen years ago I should have been a different person now."
H. J. CROPLEY, *Victoria, Australia.*

"I have gained great good

from reading the chapter 'Emergencies the Test of Ability.' You have placed my ideas of life and raised my goals far above what they once were."
RUPERT C. BOWDEN, *Magazine, Arkansas.*

Of Value to Employees

"I became so impressed with the directness of your article 'The Precedent Breaker' that I shall ask each one of our employees to read it, notifying them of its appearance through our weekly bulletin."
SAMUEL BRILL, *Head of firm of Brill Bros.*

Chapter reprinted by Bell Telephone Co.

"I take pleasure in sending you two copies of *The Telephone News*, in which appears your splendid article 'The Precedent Breaker.' We are grateful for your kind permission to send this through the *News* to six thousand Bell Telephone employees."
GEORGE G. STEEL, *Advertising Manager Bell Telephone Co. of Pennsylvania.*

An Inspiration in Time of Need

"I wish to thank you for the chapter on 'Clear Grit did It.' It has been an inspiration to me in a time when I needed it most."
C. W. HALE, *Indianapolis, Ind.*

12mo, cloth,	$1.00 net.	By mail, $1.10
Pocket Ed., silk,	1.25 net.	By mail, 1.33
Pocket Ed., leather,	1.50 net.	By mail, 1.58

THOMAS Y. CROWELL & CO., NEW YORK

Press Reviews of Dr. Marden's
Be Good to Yourself

"The author is a wonder,—

one of the very best preachers, through the pen, of our time." *Zion's Herald.*

"Just such a discussion of personality

as we all need. The titles of the chapters are appetizing and the advice and lessons taught are good. It will help many a reader to understand himself better." *The Advance.*

"The kind counsel of a new book

by Orison Swett Marden, who says there are many people who are good to others but not to themselves. This is a fine volume from every point of view." *The Religious Telescope.*

"Of a thoroughly inspirational character,

these essays are calculated to awaken and sustain the right sort of ambition and evolve a manly type of character. They are surcharged with faith, optimism, and common sense." *The Boston Herald.*

"Dr. Marden's friends,

who are to be found in all quarters of the globe, wait eagerly for such advice as this, on how to be happy, hearty, and healthy." *Seattle Post-Intelligencer.*

12mo, cloth, $1.00 net. By mail, $1.10
Pocket Ed., silk, 1.25 net. By mail, 1.33
Pocket Ed., leather, 1.50 net. By mail, 1.58

THOMAS Y. CROWELL & CO., NEW YORK

LETTERS ABOUT
Peace, Power and Plenty

"**I cannot thank you enough** for 'Peace, Power and Plenty.' Your former book, 'Every man a King,' has been my 'bedside book' for many months now,— the new one is even more of a comfort."— BLANCHE BATES.

"**I have read with great pleasure,** interest and profit your admirable 'Peace, Power and Plenty.' To have written such a book is a service to the race."— CHARLES EDWARD RUSSELL.

Andrew Carnegie says

"I thank you for 'Why Grow Old?' (a chapter in 'Peace, Power and Plenty')."

John Burroughs says

"I am reading a chapter or two in 'Peace, Power and Plenty' each evening. You preach a sound, vigorous, wholesome doctrine."

"**The most valuable chapter for me**" says Thomas Wentworth Higginson, "is that on 'Why Grow Old?' I wish to learn just that. I am now 85, and have never felt old yet, but I shall keep your chapter at hand in case that should ever happen to me."

Conan Doyle says

"I find it very stimulating and interesting."

"**The chapter on 'Health Through Right Thinking'** alone is worth five hundred dollars."— SAMUEL BRILL, Head of the firm of Brill Brothers, New York.

12mo., cloth,	*$1.00 net.*	*By mail, $1.10*
Pocket Ed., silk,	*1.25 net.*	*By mail, 1.33*
Pocket Ed., leather,	*1.50 net.*	*By mail, 1.58*

THOMAS Y. CROWELL & CO.
NEW YORK

Letters to Dr. Marden concerning

Every Man a King

Success vs. Failure

"One of the most inspiring books I have ever read. I should like to purchase a thousand and distribute them, as I believe the reading of this book would make the difference between success and failure in many lives."
CHAS. E. SCHMICK, *House of Representatives, Mass.*

Worth One Hundred Dollars

"I would not take one hundred dollars for your book, 'Every Man a King,' if no other were available."
WILLARD MERRIAM, *New York City.*

Unfailing Optimism

"The unfailing note of optimism which rings through all your works is distinctly sounded here."
W. E. HUNTINGTON, *Pres., Boston University.*

The Keynote of Life

"'Every Man a King' strikes the keynote of life. Any one of its chapters is well worth the cost of the book." E. J. TEAGARDEN, *Danbury, Conn.*

Simply Priceless

"I have just read it with tremendous interest, and I frankly say that I regard it as simply priceless. Its value to me is immeasurable, and I should be glad if I could put it in the hands of every intelligent young man and woman in this country."
CHAS. STOKES WAYNE, *Chappaqua, N. Y.*

Renewed Ambition

"I have read and re-read it with pleasure and renewed ambition. I shall ever keep it near at hand as a frequent reminder and an invaluable text-book."
H. H. WILLIAMS, *Brockton, Mass.*

12mo., cloth,	$1.00 net.	By mail, $1.10
Pocket Ed., silk,	1.25 net.	By mail, 1.33
Pocket Ed., leather,	1.50 net.	By mail, 1.58

THOMAS Y. CROWELL & CO., NEW YORK

Letters to Dr. Marden concerning

He Can Who Thinks He Can

Will Do Amazing Good

"I believe 'He Can Who Thinks He Can,' comprising some of your editorials, which appear akin to divine inspiration in words of cheer, hope, courage and success, will do amazing good."
JAMES PETER, *Independence, Kas.*

Greatest Things Ever Written

"Your editorials on the subjects of self-confidence and self-help are the greatest things ever written along that line." H. L. DUNLAP, *Waynesburg, Pa.*

Gripping Power

"Presents the truth in a remarkably clear and forcible manner, with a gripping power back of the writing. It is beautiful and inspiring."
C. W. SMELSER, *Coopertown, Okla.*

Beginning of My Success

"Your editorials have helped me more than any other reading. The beginning of my success was when I commenced to practise your teachings."
BRUCE HARTMAN, *Honolulu, T. H.*

Wishes to Reprint It

"I have been very much impressed by the chapter on 'New Thought, New Life.' I would like to send a copy of it to two thousand of my customers, giving due credit of course." JOHN D. MORRIS, *Philadelphia, Pa.*

Full of Light and Joy

"I have studied the subject of New Thought for ten years, but have never seen anything so comprehensive, so full of light and joy, as your treatment of it. When I think of the good it will do, and the thousands it will reach, my heart rejoices."
LOUISE MARKSCHEFFEL, *Toledo, O.*

12mo., cloth,	$1.00 *net.*	By mail, $1.10
Pocket Ed., silk,	1.25 *net.*	By mail, 1.33
Pocket Ed., leather,	1.50 *net.*	By mail, 1.58

THOMAS Y. CROWELL & CO., NEW YORK

Letters to Dr. Marden concerning
Pushing to the Front

What President McKinley Said

"It cannot but be an inspiration to every boy or girl who reads it, and who is possessed of an honorable and high ambition. Nothing that I have seen of late is more worthy to be placed in the hands of the American youth." WILLIAM MCKINLEY.

An English View

"I have read 'Pushing to the Front' with much interest. It would be a great stimulus to any young man entering life." SIR JOHN LUBBOCK.

A Powerful Factor

"This book has been a powerful factor in making a great change in my life. I feel that I have been born into a new world."
ROBERT S. LIVINGSTON, *Deweyville, Tex.*

The Helpfulest Book

"'Pushing to the Front' is more of a marvel to me every day. I read it almost daily. It is the helpfulest book in the English language."
MYRON T. PRITCHARD, *Boston, Mass.*

A Practical Gift

"It has been widely read by our organization of some fifteen hundred men. I have personally made presents of more than one hundred copies."
E. A. EVANS, *President Chicago Portrait Co.*

Its Weight in Gold

"If every young man could read it carefully at the beginning of his career it would be worth more to him than its weight in gold." R. T. ALLEN, *Billings, Mon.*

12mo, cloth, $1.00 net.   By mail, $1.10
Pocket Ed., silk,   1.25 net.   By mail, 1.33
Pocket Ed., leather,   1.50 net.   By mail, 1.58
Illustrated Edition, cloth, $1.50 postpaid

THOMAS Y. CROWELL COMPANY

OPINIONS OF
Rising in the World

"A storehouse of incentive,
a treasury of precious sayings; a granary of seed-thoughts capable, under proper cultivation, of a fine character harvest."—EDWARD A. HORTON.

"A stimulating book
which is pitched at a high note and rings true."
— EDWIN M. BACON.

"Has all the excellences of style
and matter that gave to 'Pushing to the Front' its signal success. Dr. Marden's power of pithy statement and pertinent illustration seems inexhaustible."— W. F. WARREN,
Former President of Boston University.

Touches the Springs of Life

"Dr. Marden has touched the springs of life and set forth with marvellous and convincing power the results obtained by those inspired by high resolves, lofty aspirations, and pure motives. No one can rise from reading this book without cleaner desires, firmer resolutions, and sublime ambition."— MYRON T. PRITCHARD,
Master of Everett School, Boston.

Its Immortal Possibilities

"Has the same iron in the blood, the same vigorous constitution, the same sanguine temperament, the same immortal possibilities as 'Pushing to the Front.'"—THOMAS W. BICKNELL,
Ex-U. S. Commissioner of Education.

12mo, cloth, $1.00 net. By mail, $1.10
Pocket Ed., silk,   1.25 net. By mail, 1.33
Pocket Ed., leather, 1.50 net. By mail, 1.58
Illustrated Edition, cloth, $1.50 postpaid

THOMAS Y. CROWELL COMPANY

PRESS REVIEWS OF
The Young Man Entering Business

"A readable volume

on a substantial topic, which discusses actual questions. The counsel of an experienced person." *Pittsburgh Post.*

Abounds in Specific Advice

"We can easily conceive that a young man who gets this book into his hands may, in after life, date his success from reading it. It is sound, wholesome, stimulating. The treatment is concrete. It abounds in specific advice and telling illustration." *Southern Observer.*

Stimulates and Encourages

"Packed as it is with sensible, practical counsels, this volume can be cordially recommended to stimulate and encourage young men starting out in business life." *Brooklyn Times.*

A Necessity to Earnest Young Men

"There is such a thing as the science of success. Dr. Marden has made a study of it. He writes in simple, attractive style. He deals with facts. The book should be in the hands of every earnest young man." *Christian Advocate.*

Entertaining as Well as Helpful

"So interwoven with personal incident and illustration that it is an entertaining as well as a helpful book." *Christian Observer.*

12mo, cloth, $1.00 net.   By mail, $1.10
Pocket Ed., silk,   1.25 net.   By mail, 1.33
Pocket Ed., leather, 1.50 net.   By mail, 1.58
Illustrated Edition, cloth, $1.50 postpaid

THOMAS Y. CROWELL COMPANY

Opinions and Reviews of Dr. Marden's
The Secret of Achievement

Exasperating

"'The Secret of Achievement' is one of those exasperating books which you feel you ought to present to your young friends, yet find yourself unwilling to part with." WILLIAM B. WARREN, *Former President Boston University.*

Art of Putting Things

"I have studied Dr. Marden's books with deep interest. He has the art of putting things; of planting in the mind convictions that will live. I know of no works that contain equal inspiration for life."
HEZEKIAH BUTTERWORTH.

A Great Service

"I thoroughly feel that you are rendering a great service to young men and women in America and throughout the world."
REV. R. S. MACARTHUR, D. D., *New York City.*

The Difference

"'Pushing to the Front' is a great book and 'Rising in the World' is a magnificent book, but 'The Secret of Achievement' is a superb book."

Success against Odds

"This volume contains a series of stimulating anecdotes and advice showing how energy, force of well-directed will, application, lofty purpose, and noble ideals serve to win success even against the greatest odds. Many a young man will draw inspiration from it which will aid him in making his life work a success."
School Journal.

12mo, cloth, $1.00 *net.* *By mail,* $1.10
Pocket Ed., silk, 1.25 *net.* *By mail,* 1.33
Pocket Ed., leather, 1.50 *net.* *By mail,* 1.58
Illustrated Edition, cloth, $1.50 *postpaid*

THOMAS Y. CROWELL COMPANY

PRESS REVIEWS OF
Talks with Great Workers

A Practical Book

"We could hardly place a more practical book than this in the hands of the young; for nothing is more fascinating than the romance of reality, the study of worthy achievement under difficulty, the contrast between obscure beginnings and triumphant endings; nothing is more valuable than to teach just such lessons as these through the medium, not of fiction, but of fact."
The Palladium.

Of Impressive Interest

"Very vividly reported and pertinent to living questions and aspirations of the hour. The volume of interviews as a whole is of impressive interest. It affords many specially interesting bits of personal opinion and experience."
New York World.

A Stimulus to Endeavor

"The book is a good one for young men and women who need a stimulus to endeavor."
Buffalo Express.

"It will pay anybody to read

in this book how representative successful people of a representatively successful age advanced to their present positions in the world. This volume is vital with interest besides being full of philosophy and practical hints." *Boston Herald.*

Of Value to the Ambitious

"Will not only prove interesting reading, but of the highest possible value to ambitious men and women striving after success."
Omaha World-Herald.

12mo, Cloth, Illustrated, $1.50

THOMAS Y. CROWELL COMPANY

PRESS REVIEWS OF
The Optimistic Life

Holds the Attention
"The title of this book attracts the attention, and the contents rivet it." *The Watchman.*

Rich in Thought and Suggestion
"A book rich in noble thought. Few are those who will not wince under the good-natured thrusts that Dr. Marden gives their foibles and weaknesses, but few also are they who may not find much helpful suggestion here."
San Francisco Chronicle.

Strengthens Spirit and Body
"Dr. Marden has done an immense amount of good by this practical advice and encouraging insistence upon the essentials of happiness. The spirit of the toiler needs strengthening quite as much as his body." *Christian Advocate.*

Its Wholesome Brain Fare
"This volume contains quantities of plain, wholesome brain fare for the misanthrope and the cynic." *Des Moines Register.*

Both Uplifting and Necessary
"'Do not look on life through smoked glasses' is Dr. Marden's motto. He believes so enthusiastically in cheerfulness, energy, and kindness that he can almost persuade one to believe there is no necessity for old age, sorrow, or discouragement. Still there is no doubt but his message is not only uplifting but necessary."
Indianapolis News.

12mo, cloth, $1.00 *net.* *By mail,* $1.10
Pocket Ed., silk, 1.25 *net.* *By mail,* 1.33
Pocket Ed., leather, 1.50 *net.* *By mail,* 1.58
Illustrated Edition, cloth, $1.50 *postpaid*

THOMAS Y. CROWELL COMPANY

BOOK JUNGLE

Bringing Classics to Life

www.bookjungle.com email: sales@bookjungle.com fax: 630-214-0564 mail: Book Jungle PO Box 2226 Champaign, IL 61825

The Two Babylons
Alexander Hislop
You may be surprised to learn that many traditions of Roman Catholicism in fact don't come from Christ's teachings but from an ancient Babylonian "Mystery" religion that was centered on Nimrod, his wife Semiramis, and a child Tammuz. This book shows how this ancient religion transformed itself as it incorporated Christ into its teachings ...

Religion/History   Pages:358

ISBN: *1-59462-010-5*   MSRP *$22.95*

QTY

The Go-Getter
Kyne B. Peter
The Go Getter is the story of William Peck. He was a war veteran and amputee who will not be refused what he wants. Peck not only fights to find employment but continually proves himself more than competent at the many difficult test that are throw his way in the course of his early days with the Ricks Lumber Company ..

Business/Self Help/Inspirational   Pages:68

ISBN: *1-59462-186-1*   MSRP *$8.95*

QTY

The Power Of Concentration
Theron Q. Dumont
It is of the utmost value to learn how to concentrate. To make the greatest success of anything you must be able to concentrate your entire thought upon the idea you are working on. The person that is able to concentrate utilizes all constructive thoughts and shuts out all destructive ones...

Self Help/Inspirational   Pages:196

ISBN: *1-59462-141-1*   MSRP *$14.95*

Self Mastery
Emile Coue
Emile Coue came up with novel way to improve the lives of people. He was a pharmacist by trade and often saw ailing people. This lead him to develop autosuggestion, a form of self-hypnosis. At the time his theories weren't popular but over the years evidence is mounting that he was indeed right all along ..

New Age/Self Help   Pages:98

ISBN: *1-59462-189-6*   MSRP *$7.95*

Rightly Dividing The Word
Clarence Larkin
The "Fundamental Doctrines" of the Christian Faith are clearly outlined in numerous books on Theology, but they are not available to the average reader and were mainly written for students. The Author has made it the work of his ministry to preach the "Fundamental Doctrines." To this end he has aimed to express them in the simplest and clearest manner..

Religion   Pages:352

ISBN: *1-59462-334-1*   MSRP *$23.45*

The Awful Disclosures Of
Maria Monk
"I cannot banish the scenes and characters of this book from my memory. To me it can never appear like an amusing fable, or lose its interest and importance. The story is one which is continually before me, and must return fresh to my mind with painful emotions as long as I live.."

Religion   Pages:232

ISBN: *1-59462-160-8*   MSRP *$17.95*

The Law of Psychic Phenomena
Thomson Jay Hudson
"I do not expect this book to stand upon its literary merits; for if it is unsound in principle, felicity of diction cannot save it, and if sound, homeliness of expression cannot destroy it. My primary object in offering it to the public is to assist in bringing Psychology within the domain of the exact sciences. That this has never been accomplished..."

New Age   Pages:420

ISBN: *1-59462-124-1*   MSRP *$29.95*

As a Man Thinketh
James Allen
"This little volume (the result of meditation and experience) is not intended as an exhaustive treatise on the much-written-upon subject of the power of thought. It is suggestive rather than explanatory, its object being to stimulate men and women to the discovery and perception of the truth that by virtue of the thoughts which they choose and encourage..."

Inspirational/Self Help   Pages:80

ISBN: *1-59462-231-0*   MSRP *$9.45*

Beautiful Joe
Marshall Saunders
When Marshall visited the Moore family in 1892, she discovered Joe, a dog that had nursed back to health from his previous abusive home to live a happy life. So moved was she, that she wrote this classic masterpiece which won accolades and was recognized as a heartwarming symbol for humane animal treatment...

Fiction   Pages:256

ISBN: *1-59462-261-2*   MSRP *$18.45*

The Enchanted April
Elizabeth Von Arnim
It began in a woman's club in London on a February afternoon, an uncomfortable club, and a miserable afternoon when Mrs. Wilkins, who had come down from Hampstead to shop and had lunched at her club, took up The Times from the table in the smoking-room...

Fiction   Pages:368

ISBN: *1-59462-150-0*   MSRP *$23.45*

The Codes Of Hammurabi And
Moses - W. W. Davies
The discovery of the Hammurabi Code is one of the greatest achievements of archaeology, and is of paramount interest, not only to the student of the Bible, but also to all those interested in ancient history...

Religion   Pages:132

ISBN: *1-59462-338-4*   MSRP *$12.95*

Holland - The History Of Netherlands
Thomas Colley Grattan
Thomas Grattan was a prestigious writer from Dublin who served as British Consul to the US. Among his works is an authoritative look at the history of Holland. A colorful and interesting look at history....

History/Politics   Pages:408

ISBN: *1-59462-137-3*   MSRP *$26.95*

The Thirty-Six Dramatic Situations
Georges Polti
An incredibly useful guide for aspiring authors and playwrights. This volume categorizes every dramatic situation which could occur in a story and describes them in a list of 36 situations. A great aid to help inspire or formalize the creative writing process...

Self Help/Reference   Pages:204

ISBN: *1-59462-134-9*   MSRP *$15.95*

A Concise Dictionary of Middle English
A. L. Mayhew
Walter W. Skeat
The present work is intended to meet, in some measure, the requirements of those who wish to make some study of Middle-English, and who find a difficulty in obtaining such assistance as will enable them to find out the meanings and etymologies of the words most essential to their purpose...

Reference/History   Pages:332

ISBN: *1-59462-119-5*   MSRP *$29.95*

www.bookjungle.com email: sales@bookjungle.com fax: 630-214-0564 mail: Book Jungle PO Box 2226 Champaign, IL 61825

BOOK JUNGLE

Bringing Classics to Life

www.bookjungle.com email: sales@bookjungle.com fax: 630-214-0564 mail: Book Jungle PO Box 2226 Champaign, IL 61825

The Witch-Cult in Western Europe
Margaret Murray   QTY

The mass of existing material on this subject is so great that I have not attempted to make a survey of the whole of European "Witchcraft" but have confined myself to an intensive study of the cult in Great Britain. In order, however, to obtain a clearer understanding of the ritual and beliefs I have had recourse to French and Flemish sources...

Occult   Pages:308
ISBN: 1-59462-126-8   MSRP $22.45

Philosophy Of Natural Therapeutics
Henry Lindlahr   QTY

We invite the earnest cooperation in this great work of all those who have awakened to the necessity for more rational living and for radical reform in healing methods...

Health/Philosophy/Self Help   Pages:552
ISBN: 1-59462-132-2   MSRP $34.95

The Science Of Psychic Healing
Yogi Ramacharaka

This book is not a book of theories it deals with facts. Its author regards the best of theories as but working hypotheses to be used only until better ones present themselves. The "fact" is the principal thing the essential thing to uncover which the tool, theory, is used...

New Age/Health   Pages:180
ISBN: 1-59462-140-3   MSRP $13.95

A Message to Garcia
Elbert Hubbard

This literary trifle, A Message to Garcia, was written one evening after supper, in a single hour. It was on the Twenty-second of February, Eighteen Hundred Ninety-nine, Washington's Birthday, and we were just going to press with the March Philistine...

New Age/Fiction   Pages:92
ISBN: 1-59462-144-6   MSRP $9.95

Bible Myths
Thomas Doane

In pursuing the study of the Bible Myths, facts pertaining thereto, in a condensed form, seemed to be greatly needed, and nowhere to be found. Widely scattered through hundreds of ancient and modern volumes, most of the contents of this book may indeed be found; but any previous attempt to trace exclusively the myths and legends...

Religion/History   Pages:644
ISBN: 1-59462-163-2   MSRP $38.95

The Book of Jasher
Alcuinus Flaccus Albinus

The Book of Jasher is an historical religious volume that many consider as a missing holy book from the Old Testament. Particularly studied by the Church of Later Day Saints and historians, it covers the history of the world from creation until the period of Judges in Israel. It's authenticity is bolstered due to a reference to the Book of Jasher in the Bible in Joshua 10:13

Religion/History   Pages:276
ISBN: 1-59462-197-7   MSRP $18.95

Tertium Organum
P. D. Ouspensky

A truly mind expanding writing that combines science with mysticism with unprecedented elegance. He presents the world we live in as a multi dimensional world and time as a motion through this world. But this isn't a cold and purely analytical explanation but a masterful presentation filled with similes and analogies...

New Age   Pages:356
ISBN: 1-59462-205-1   MSRP $23.95

The Titan
Theodore Dreiser

"When Frank Algernon Cowperwood emerged from the Eastern District Penitentiary, in Philadelphia he realized that the old life he had lived in that city since boyhood was ended. His youth was gone, and with it had been lost the great business prospects of his earlier manhood. He must begin again..."

Fiction   Pages:564
ISBN: 1-59462-220-5   MSRP $33.95

Advance Course in Yogi Philosophy
Yogi Ramacharaka

"The twelve lessons forming this volume were originally issued in the shape of monthly lessons, known as "The Advanced Course in Yogi Philosophy and Oriental Occultism" during a period of twelve months beginning with October, 1904, and ending September, 1905."

Philosophy/Inspirational/Self Help Pages:340
ISBN: 1-59462-229-9   MSRP $22.95

Biblical Essays
J. B. Lightfoot

About one-third of the present volume has already seen the light. The opening essay "On the Internal Evidence for the Authenticity and Genuineness of St John's Gospel" was published in the "Expositor" in the early months of 1890, and has been reprinted since...

Religion/History   Pages:480
ISBN: 1-59462-238-8   MSRP $30.95

Ambassador Morgenthau's Story
Henry Morgenthau

"By this time the American people have probably become convinced that the Germans deliberately planned the conquest of the world. Yet they hesitate to convict on circumstantial evidence and for this reason all eye witnesses to this, the greatest crime in modern history, should volunteer their testimony..."

History   Pages:472
ISBN: 1-59462-244-2   MSRP $29.95

The Settlement Cook Book
Simon Kander

A legacy from the civil war, this book is a classic "American charity cookbook," which was used for fundraisers starting in Milwaukee. While it has transformed over the years, this printing provides great recipes from American history. Over two million copies have been sold. This volume contains a rich collection of recipes from noted chefs and hostesses of the turn of the century...

How-to   Pages:472
ISBN: 1-59462-256-6   MSRP $29.95

The Aquarian Gospel of Jesus the Christ
Levi Dowling

A retelling of Jesus' story which tells us what happened during the twenty year gap left by the Bible's New Testament. It tells of his travels to the far-east where he studied with the masters and fought against the rigid caste system. This book has enjoyed a resurgence in modern America and provides spiritual insight with charm. Its influences can be seen throughout the Age of Aquarius.

Religion   Pages:264
ISBN: 1-59462-321-X   MSRP $18.95

My Life and Work
Henry Ford

Henry Ford revolutionized the world with his implementation of mass production for the Model T automobile. Gain valuable business insight into his life and work with his own auto-biography... "We have only started on our development of our country have not as yet, with all our talk of wonderful progress, done more than scratch the surface. The progress has been wonderful enough but..."

Biographies/History/Business   Pages:300
ISBN: 1-59462-198-5   MSRP $21.95

www.bookjungle.com email: sales@bookjungle.com fax: 630-214-0564 mail: Book Jungle PO Box 2226 Champaign, IL 61825

BOOK JUNGLE

Bringing Classics to Life

www.bookjungle.com email: sales@bookjungle.com fax: 630-214-0564 mail: Book Jungle PO Box 2226 Champaign, IL 61825

QTY

The Rosicrucian Cosmo-Conception Mystic Christianity by Max Heindel	ISBN: 1-59462-188-8	$38.95

The Rosicrucian Cosmo-conception is not dogmatic, neither does it appeal to any other authority than the reason of the student. It is: not controversial, but is: sent forth in the, hope that it may help to clear...
New Age/Religion Pages 646

Abandonment To Divine Providence by Jean-Pierre de Caussade	ISBN: 1-59462-228-0	$25.95

"The Rev. Jean Pierre de Caussade was one of the most remarkable spiritual writers of the Society of Jesus in France in the 18th Century. His death took place at Toulouse in 1751. His works have gone through many editions and have been republished...
Inspirational/Religion Pages 400

Mental Chemistry by Charles Haanel	ISBN: 1-59462-192-6	$23.95

Mental Chemistry allows the change of material conditions by combining and appropriately utilizing the power of the mind. Much like applied chemistry creates something new and unique out of careful combinations of chemicals the mastery of mental chemistry...
New Age Pages 354

The Letters of Robert Browning and Elizabeth Barret Barrett 1845-1846 vol II by Robert Browning and Elizabeth Barrett	ISBN: 1-59462-193-4	$35.95

Biographies Pages 596

Gleanings In Genesis (volume I) by Arthur W. Pink	ISBN: 1-59462-130-6	$27.45

Appropriately has Genesis been termed "the seed plot of the Bible" for in it we have, in germ form, almost all of the great doctrines which are afterwards fully developed in the books of Scripture which follow...
Religion/Inspirational Pages 420

The Master Key by L. W. de Laurence	ISBN: 1-59462-001-6	$30.95

In no branch of human knowledge has there been a more lively increase of the spirit of research during the past few years than in the study of Psychology, Concentration and Mental Discipline. The requests for authentic lessons in Thought Control, Mental Discipline and...
New Age/Business Pages 422

The Lesser Key Of Solomon Goetia by L. W. de Laurence	ISBN: 1-59462-092-X	$9.95

This translation of the first book of the "Lemegeton" which is now for the first time made accessible to students of Talismanic Magic was done, after careful collation and edition, from numerous Ancient Manuscripts in Hebrew, Latin, and French...
New Age/Occult Pages 92

Rubaiyat Of Omar Khayyam by Edward Fitzgerald	ISBN: 1-59462-332-5	$13.95

Edward Fitzgerald, whom the world has already learned, in spite of his own efforts to remain within the shadow of anonymity, to look upon as one of the rarest poets of the century, was born at Bredfield, in Suffolk, on the 31st of March, 1809. He was the third son of John Purcell...
Music Pages 172

Ancient Law by Henry Maine	ISBN: 1-59462-128-4	$29.95

The chief object of the following pages is to indicate some of the earliest ideas of mankind, as they are reflected in Ancient Law, and to point out the relation of those ideas to modern thought.
Religion/History Pages 452

Far-Away Stories by William J. Locke	ISBN: 1-59462-129-2	$19.45

"Good wine needs no bush, but a collection of mixed vintages does. And this book is just such a collection. Some of the stories I do not want to remain buried for ever in the museum files of dead magazine-numbers an author's not unpardonable vanity..."
Fiction Pages 272

Life of David Crockett by David Crockett	ISBN: 1-59462-250-7	$27.45

"Colonel David Crockett was one of the most remarkable men of the times in which he lived. Born in humble life, but gifted with a strong will, an indomitable courage, and unremitting perseverance...
Biographies/New Age Pages 424

Lip-Reading by Edward Nitchie	ISBN: 1-59462-206-X	$25.95

Edward B. Nitchie, founder of the New York School for the Hard of Hearing, now the Nitchie School of Lip-Reading, Inc, wrote "LIP-READING Principles and Practice". The development and perfecting of this meritorious work on lip-reading was an undertaking...
How-to Pages 400

A Handbook of Suggestive Therapeutics, Applied Hypnotism, Psychic Science by Henry Munro	ISBN: 1-59462-214-0	$24.95

Health/New Age/Health/Self-help Pages 376

A Doll's House; and Two Other Plays by Henrik Ibsen	ISBN: 1-59462-112-8	$19.95

Henrik Ibsen created this classic when in revolutionary 1848 Rome. Introducing some striking concepts in playwriting for the realist genre, this play has been studied the world over.
Fiction/Classics/Plays 308

The Light of Asia by sir Edwin Arnold	ISBN: 1-59462-204-3	$13.95

In this poetic masterpiece, Edwin Arnold describes the life and teachings of Buddha. The man who was to become known as Buddha to the world was born as Prince Gautama of India but he rejected the worldly riches and abandoned the reigns of power when...
Religion/History/Biographies Pages 170

The Complete Works of Guy de Maupassant by Guy de Maupassant	ISBN: 1-59462-157-8	$16.95

"For days and days, nights and nights, I had dreamed of that first kiss which was to consecrate our engagement, and I knew not on what spot I should put my lips..."
Fiction/Classics Pages 240

The Art of Cross-Examination by Francis L. Wellman	ISBN: 1-59462-309-0	$26.95

Written by a renowned trial lawyer, Wellman imparts his experience and uses case studies to explain how to use psychology to extract desired information through questioning.
How-to/Science/Reference Pages 408

Answered or Unanswered? by Louisa Vaughan	ISBN: 1-59462-248-5	$10.95

Miracles of Faith in China
Religion Pages 112

The Edinburgh Lectures on Mental Science (1909) by Thomas	ISBN: 1-59462-008-3	$11.95

This book contains the substance of a course of lectures recently given by the writer in the Queen Street Hall, Edinburgh. Its purpose is to indicate the Natural Principles governing the relation between Mental Action and Material Conditions...
New Age/Psychology Pages 148

Ayesha by H. Rider Haggard	ISBN: 1-59462-301-5	$24.95

Verily and indeed it is the unexpected that happens! Probably if there was one person upon the earth from whom the Editor of this, and of a certain previous history, did not expect to hear again...
Classics Pages 380

Ayala's Angel by Anthony Trollope	ISBN: 1-59462-352-X	$29.95

The two girls were both pretty, but Lucy who was twenty-one who supposed to be simple and comparatively unattractive, whereas Ayala was credited, as her Bombwhat romantic name might show, with poetic charm and a taste for romance. Ayala when her father died was nineteen...
Fiction Pages 484

The American Commonwealth by James Bryce	ISBN: 1-59462-286-8	$34.45

An interpretation of American democratic political theory. It examines political mechanics and society from the perspective of Scotsman James Bryce
Politics Pages 572

Stories of the Pilgrims by Margaret P. Pumphrey	ISBN: 1-59462-116-0	$17.95

This book explores pilgrims religious oppression in England as well as their escape to Holland and eventual crossing to America on the Mayflower, and their early days in New England.
History Pages 268

www.bookjungle.com email: sales@bookjungle.com fax: 630-214-0564 mail: Book Jungle PO Box 2226 Champaign, IL 61825

BOOK JUNGLE

Bringing Classics to Life

www.bookjungle.com email: sales@bookjungle.com fax: 630-214-0564 mail: Book Jungle PO Box 2226 Champaign, IL 61825

			QTY
The Fasting Cure by **Sinclair Upton**	ISBN: *1-59462-222-1*	**$13.95**	☐
In the Cosmopolitan Magazine for May, 1910, and in the Contemporary Review (London) for April, 1910, I published an article dealing with my experiences in fasting. I have written a great many magazine articles, but never one which attracted so much attention... New Age/Self Help/Health Pages 164			
Hebrew Astrology by **Sepharial**	ISBN: *1-59462-308-2*	**$13.45**	☐
In these days of advanced thinking it is a matter of common observation that we have left many of the old landmarks behind and that we are now pressing forward to greater heights and to a wider horizon than that which represented the mind-content of our progenitors... Astrology Pages 144			
Thought Vibration or The Law of Attraction in the Thought World	ISBN: *1-59462-127-6*	**$12.95**	☐
by William Walker Atkinson	Psychology/Religion Pages 144		
Optimism by **Helen Keller**	ISBN: *1-59462-108-X*	**$15.95**	☐
Helen Keller was blind, deaf, and mute since 19 months old, yet famously learned how to overcome these handicaps, communicate with the world, and spread her lectures promoting optimism. An inspiring read for everyone... Biographies/Inspirational Pages 84			
Sara Crewe by **Frances Burnett**	ISBN: *1-59462-360-0*	**$9.45**	☐
In the first place, Miss Minchin lived in London. Her home was a large, dull, tall one, in a large, dull square, where all the houses were alike, and all the sparrows were alike, and where all the door-knockers made the same heavy sound... Childrens/Classic Pages 88			
The Autobiography of Benjamin Franklin by **Benjamin Franklin**	ISBN: *1-59462-135-7*	**$24.95**	☐
The Autobiography of Benjamin Franklin has probably been more extensively read than any other American historical work, and no other book of its kind has had such ups and downs of fortune. Franklin lived for many years in England, where he was agent... Biographies/History Pages 332			

Name	
Email	
Telephone	
Address	
City, State ZIP	

☐ Credit Card   ☐ Check / Money Order

Credit Card Number	
Expiration Date	
Signature	

Please Mail to: Book Jungle
                  PO Box 2226
                  Champaign, IL 61825
or Fax to: 630-214-0564

ORDERING INFORMATION

web: www.bookjungle.com
email: sales@bookjungle.com
fax: 630-214-0564
mail: Book Jungle PO Box 2226 Champaign, IL 61825
or PayPal to sales@bookjungle.com

Please contact us for bulk discounts

DIRECT-ORDER TERMS

**20% Discount if You Order
Two or More Books**
Free Domestic Shipping!
Accepted: Master Card, Visa,
Discover, American Express

www.bookjungle.com email: sales@bookjungle.com fax: 630-214-0564 mail: Book Jungle PO Box 2226 Champaign, IL 61825

www.ingramcontent.com/pod-product-compliance
Lightning Source LLC
Chambersburg PA
CBHW081211230426
43666CB00015B/2717